JUST A TINY PRICK

Geoffrey Hackett

The rise and rise of a "Sex Tsar".

The title "Sex Tsar" as awarded to me by a Men's Health journalist in 2005, during an article on the health benefits on sex. Throughout my career, I have always struggled to find a title that describes, precisely, my unique interests, insights, and skills that I have acquired over the last 30 years. I felt the term "Sex Tsar", captured this rather nicely, if somewhat humorously grandiose. I now wear the badge with pride.

Professor Geoffrey Hackett

Contents

Dedications

- The late Dr Graham Jackson "the man who knew too much" – my greatest inspiration and the finest physician of his time.
- Professor Mike Kirby "font of all knowledge" – a great friend, collaborator, and fitness fanatic.
- Professor Alan Riley, the Father of Sexual Medicine in the UK.
- Dr Bollinger for being "larger than life, inspirational and a generous friend and provider of many memorable moments.
- Mr Mike Heal, a Urologist from Crewe, who first showed me how to produce an erection.
- Mr Amged El-Hawrani, Consultant ENT surgeon and my appraiser in 2019 and 2020, and tragic victim of Covid-19 on 28th March 2020.
- Julie Spinks, my long-suffering hospital secretary.
- Bob Stokes (bob@bobstokes.co.uk) for the excellent cartoons.
- And not least,
- My wife Sally, for over 40 years of support of the "Sex Tsar" ... and counting.
- I have attempted to respect the privacy of colleagues and patients who might not wish to be identified. Dates and times have been altered to prevent identification, along with certain details that might have allowed recognition of various scenarios.

Introduction

Recent years have seen the growth of public interest in medical autobiographies. These often reveal behind the scenes activities, which are a mixture of fascination, information, amusement, and at times, sadness. It is also a way of providing insights into particular areas of medicine. An excellent example was the best seller "This is going to hurt" by Adam Kay, published in 2017. His title clearly reflects a common warning given to patients prior to medical procedures. Similarly, as a sex doctor "Just a tiny prick" is a phrase I commonly use prior to injections in a delicate area, although, based on some patient responses, I tend to avoid the phrase nowadays.

Another reason for writing this book is that sexual problems have always been difficult for people, and men in particular, to talk about. Such issues carry a lot of shame and fear but unaddressed they lead to unhappiness and misery. While it is certainly the case that people can read academic books about the nature of erectile dysfunction, premature ejaculation, or vaginismus (vaginal spasm), learning about these issues through other people's stories can have more impact. I have had 30 years' experience working in urology and sexual medicine and seen nearly every sexual problem imaginable. I have even pioneered certain treatments such as daily use of medications for erectile dysfunction and testosterone therapy in diabetes. There have been many controversies as not all of my colleagues agree on the diagnosis or treatment of certain conditions. When it comes to sexual problems, everybody has an opinion. As I enter the twilight years of my career, it is time to look back and reflect on the many patients that I have helped through difficult times and share my insights. I believe in this book. I hope it will be popular, be informative, guide people through difficult times, and most of all, sell many copies.

My story begins with my first clinic in sexual medicine practice, over 27 years ago. in much the same way as crime films often start with the gruesome murder and then builds the tension with flashbacks over several years. I chose to use this method in the narrative by getting the tasty stuff in early to grab and, hopefully hold the attention. In later chapters, I deal with early years of education, in Australia, the UK, and Kings College Hospital Medical School from 1968-1974. I will move on to years as a junior hospital doctor from 1974-78, a GP partner from 1978 to 2005 and a Consultant in Sexual Medicine and Urology from 1993 to the present day. Along the way I also reached the heights of Professor in Sexual Medicine. There are chapters on attendances at sex conferences around the world, fascinating medical research into sexual problems and interesting media appearances.

The final chapter entitled "serious stuff" focuses on what we can all do to improve our sex-lives, sexual health, general health, and happiness – the sort of insight and advice that you will probably never learn from your own doctor. In 2020, we learned from Diabetes UK that, in the last 20 years, the number of people with obesity has increased from 6.9 to 13 million, and this accounts for 85% of the risk of developing type 2 diabetes. Current NHS strategies are clearly failing, and, in this chapter, I will lay out the evidence for alternative approaches current being ignored by the NHS, who are obsessed by sugar and fat, continually placing blame on the individual for poor diet and lack of exercise.

Whereas most doctors like to pretend that they planned every stage of their medical career, in all honesty mine was a series of chance events. Despite that, there is little that I would change, apart from passing the exams that I failed. Although this book focuses on the junior hospital life of the 70s, where the 95-hour weeks described by Adam Kay would have seemed like utopia, it also describes a golden age of general practice, when there was time to talk with patients and the GP was a trusted friend. My evolution into what the Daily Mail termed a "Sex Tsar" happened purely by chance. I feel very lucky to have been in at the very beginning and travelled the world to International Conferences and on Speaker Tours. I have also been involved in some of the most bizarre clinical trials, as will become evident to the reader. I have met many wonderful patients and colleagues along the way. Hopefully, most of them will remain friends after they read these chapters.

The final push to write this book came from an unsolicited letter sent to me by an eminent urologist from Norway, which read:

Sir!

I would like to thank for all your brilliant publications on diabetes, Erectile Dysfunction, and the heart!

Being a urologist, I am struggling hard to convince my fellow colleagues in Norway about the importance of correcting male hypogonadism not only to improve sexual function, but also metabolic status and risk of Heart Disease.

Your recent review on metabolic effects of testosterone therapy in men with Type 2 Diabetes in Journal of Sexual Medicine (2019) should be compulsory reading for all doctors and medical students. Not only does it stand out as academically brilliant, it also has literary qualities that remind me of the author of not-so-academic-books Terry Pratchett, who is one of my favourites.

I am your biggest fan!

I thought to myself "wow" Terry Pratchett, there might be some talent there after all! The enforced self-isolation during the Covid-19 crisis provided the crucial time needed for putting pen to paper as even the sex tsar was not required for front line clinical contact during that period. I did, however, volunteer to return to the NHS to help with telephone and video consultations during the crisis.

The hardest question I have faced in later years has been "What type of doctor are you?" I used to try the term "Andrologist" but invariably I would get questions about technical problems with mobile phones or questions about star signs. Sometimes on holidays, I would dread the question, as most people seem the to have a "friend" with a sexual problem. On a recent Safari holiday in South Africa I posed as a taxidermist for the entire week on the basis that most people would have no friends who required "stuffing". My cunning plan lasted until the last night until my wife mentioned at dinner that she had just received a text asking whether I would be speaking at the World Association of Sexology (WAS) meeting next month. On overhearing this, one of the group commented "What do sexologists want with a f*****g taxidermist?" My cover was blown and within 10 minutes he was telling me about a "friend" with an embarrassing curvature.

The term "Sex Tsar" has worked wonders on my Tinder account, as anybody seeking this as an essential quality could readily discover me as the answer to their dreams.

CHAPTER 1 – The Rise of the Sex Tsar

This chapter charts the development of the Erectile Dysfunction Clinic at Good Hope Hospital in Sutton Coldfield and case histories of couples attending. It highlights the importance of sex, especially in older men seeking new relationships in later life, demonstrating that there is more to look forward to than Countdown, cocoa, and an early night. I make no apologies for getting straight into some top tumescent tales.

CHAPTER 2 – Early Education and Medical School Years

What were the signs from early and medical school education that the Sex Tsar was to emerge? Without doubt these are the best years of our lives, but we do not realise this at the time. Certainly, London Medical Schools in the 1970s were vibrant places, apart from gynaecology clinics in Brixton on hot summer afternoons. It is difficult to believe that some of the stories described in this chapter really did happen.

CHAPTER 3 - Junior Hospital Doctor Years

Tyrannical Consultants insisting on 24/7 on call rotas, falling asleep through exhaustion during operations, rats in the on-call quarters, these were really tough times. Tell that to junior doctors today and they do not believe you. The Tsar describes a number of surgical disasters and close shaves that would never happen today, or would they? Could a porter really administer anaesthetics for years without being noticed? Could a man really wedge a TV aerial up his rectum simply by seeking better reception? The answers are in this chapter.

CHAPTER 4 - Viagra Years and Beyond

The Sex Tsar explains the incredible story of the development of the most famous drug in the world and how it changed medical practice. You will learn the details of the sexual practices of a precision grinder and the risks of running a 4x 100m relay after taking a dose of Viagra. There are key messages for those of you with body image concerns or those contemplating genital piercing.

CHAPTER 5 - The Sex Tsar and the Media

The media constantly seek the Sex Tsar for media work. This chapter explains the benefits of sex to recharge lust levels. Media training courses will not be required if you follow the Tsar's five top tips for dealing with the press and TV. This chapter also contains helpful advice on the sex benefits of antique furniture and training tips for aspiring world masturbation champions.

CHAPTER 6 – International Travel with the Sex Tsar

With the future of international travel uncertain, what could be better than travelling to exotic locations with the Sex Tsar? You might never have contemplated international travel with a large set of buttocks or considered the best batter for Korean tempura dog's testicles. The Sex Tsar provides top tips. You will learn the best way to handle the common embarrassing situation of being locked out of your hotel room stark naked, the correct way of tipping your female golf caddy in Indonesia, and how to deal with common mid-air medical emergencies. This chapter is the complete almanac for international jetsetters.

CHAPTER 7 – The Sex Tsar in General Practice

Nothing is hospital medicine can prepare a doctor for what awaits them as a country general practitioner. Whether it is dealing with cardiac arrests in remote areas, psychopaths brandishing Arabic swords, or simply knowing where to store your thermometer when visiting nudist colonies, this chapter has helpful tips for all occasions.

CHAPTER 8 – The Sex Tsar in Clinical Research

The Tsar has conducted multiple original research projects for both men and women and the findings are revealed here. The reader will learn how to master the controls of the ejaculometer, the preferred positions for sex in a MRI scanner, or the medical benefits of fellatio. The more bizarre the project, the more likely that the reader should be able to get a grant. Next year one of my readers might be presenting at the Scandinavian Society for the Study of Sexual Statistics.

CHAPTER 9 – The Serious Stuff

This is the most important chapter in the book. The Tsar has condensed 30 years of experience into this single chapter. If you read this and follow the take home messages, no other books or magazines on health will be required. Sex is fundamental to good health and relationships are crucial to human happiness. Every erection, orgasm and ejaculation should be a cause for celebration and sex should be enjoyed at least 3 times per week for maximum benefit, fully endorsed by a medical certificate from the tsar. He explains why you cannot expect your GP to look after all aspects of your health, as, contractually they are working to a different agenda. We need to become masters of our own health and "the Serious Stuff" tells you precisely what needs to be done. This chapter includes important information relevant to the Covid 19 pandemic and possible future pandemics.

CHAPTER 1.
The Rise of the Sex Tsar

Well, stories have to start somewhere and, in my case, it begins at 6.30 pm on Tuesday 14th December 1994. My Erectile Dysfunction (ED) Clinic at Good Hope Hospital in Sutton Coldfield was really getting up a head of steam after a sluggish start. The original idea was that the clinic was set up to deal with problems in men and women but for political and logistic reasons the clinical commissioners decided not to cover female referrals. I wondered what had been done for all these men (and indeed women) with sexual problems before I started. The reality was nothing at all. I had seen about 20 patients and was just about ready for home, when the clinic clerk told me that Mr John Thomas (not his real name of course) had returned after his treatment 4 hours earlier. This was some 4 years before the availability of Viagra, but more about that later. At that time, treatment usually consisted of an injection in the penis with a drug called papaverine, although we had recently started using alprostadil as a special mixture made up in the pharmacy at Leighton Hospital, Crewe, under a government licence.

My "Road to Damascus" moment had occurred in 1988, when, as a GP, I carried out a couple of vasectomies with Mike Heal, a Urologist at Leighton Hospital, Crewe. I was looking for ways to boost my GP earnings, but I rapidly learned that vasectomy was a very hard way to make money. Throughout the procedures, I was constantly reminded why I decided against a career in surgery. By chance, Mr Heal was called back to outpatients to review a man who had been injected in the penis earlier that day. The sight of that large bender was like a flash of light. I had discovered my calling. A random event had changed my life.

This method of injection treatment gained popularity in the mid-80s, when a famous British Urologist, Giles Brindley, famously injected himself on stage at an International Urology meeting in Las Vegas. Nobody had informed him that his prestigious lecture was being attended by the wives of several eminent American Urologists when he chose to expose his impressive erection on stage. Several ladies fainted and others were treated for shock.

John Thomas was in his late 60s. He suffered from high blood pressure and raised cholesterol and had been alone for several years, after a traumatic divorce. He had just met Doris, 62, and recently widowed, at a local tea dance. In his own words, they both had a "lot of catching up to do". It was clear that neither had been looking for long evenings by the fireside, watching Countdown and Deal or no Deal. He wanted action, and quickly. Initially the suggestion of an injection into his penis prior to sex was not something that he had contemplated but he was prepared to "give it a go".

The problem in 1994 was that none of us were certain what dose to use for this first test. If we used too little and with no sexual stimulation, then most men might lose heart. I was unsure of the starting dose for Mr Thomas but luckily, I had been to a seminal lecture a few weeks earlier from Mr Clive Gingell, an eminent Bristol Urologist and I had posed this very question to him. I remember his answer to this day:

"Well, Dr Hackett, that is a very good question, and this is the way I approach it. I normally start with 10 micrograms but

If I have a young man with little in the way of medical problems, then I might give 5 micrograms, if, on the other hand, I have a man with severe diabetes, I might start with 20. Sometimes there is no alternative but to just suck it and see!"

Although I never fancied taking up his last piece of advice, in the case of JT, and his search for a fast start, I went for 20 micrograms. As he undressed, he made the very familiar comment "it's a cold day, I'm afraid it's rather small". I tended to agree but made light of the diminutive size and delivered a full dose of 20 micrograms.

We were all aware of the need for sexual stimulation to augment the effect of any medication, so, in the early days, I provided several copies of Playboy that I had found under the bed of an ex-roommate. Unfortunately, these were never returned to the clinic. I had been reduced to subscribing to the Sun and leaving copies open at page 3 in the examination rooms. I still mourn the absence of page 3 girls. I still blame the rise of the feminist movement.

The response to the injection was almost instantaneous, with a quite splendid erection. "My word" he gasped, "that is really the most impressive thing I have ever seen" and left the clinic cock-a-hoop.

Now 4 hours later he was back in considerable discomfort. Doris was at the hairdressers all afternoon and despite several attempts at masturbation and watching a 1-hour Fanny Craddock cookery special, it had not gone down. He felt that his penis was "on fire" and might explode any second. He was in agony and crying with excruciating pain. He dropped his trousers to reveal a throbbing rock- hard priapism. I have realised that, in this situation, a man would willingly give all his money, his wife, his house, his Aston Villa season ticket, anything to be relieved. I inserted the largest size needles I could find into both sides of the throbbing mass and dark blood began to run out into the dish. "Ahhhhhh..." he uttered – the relief was palpable. He was the first patient ever to offer me a tip for services provided. Half an hour later, suitably deflated, he went home. I realised that his future follow- up might not be quite as straight forward but that was a problem for another day. Clearly, in his case, I should probably have adopted the "suck it and see" approach.

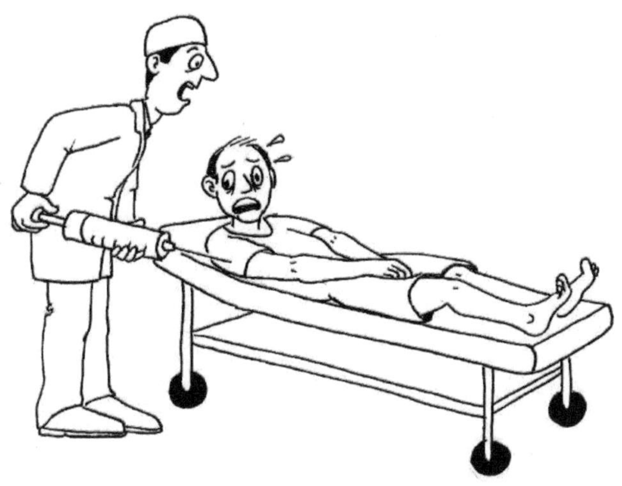

"The dose? Sometimes I just have to suck it and see."

Around this time, I was involved in a weekend conference with a famous female Urologist, Christine Evans, teaching GPs about ED. UK urologists would agree that Christine was definitely "one of a kind". She explained to the audience that she liked to give the men of North Wales a good priapism, so they knew "what it felt like". This was because of the remoteness of the area, meaning that emergency services were limited. She also suggested that she only treated older men if they had an attractive younger partner. I had to hastily add that I could not endorse either of these views. Christine later became a TV celebrity on "Under the knife with Dr Christine" but for me, her finest moment was an appearance on BBC TV "The Celebrity Weakest Link" with Anne Robinson, where she was narrowly beaten in a final question decider about a member of the cast of Emmerdale. Her victorious opponent was none other than Basil Brush. The thrilling conclusion of that particular episode is still available on You Tube.

It was December 21st, 1994 and my first appointment was a 72-year-old Irishman, James O'Flaherty. He has been widowed for 12 years but has just moved into a retirement apartment where he was the only male. His first wife was staunch Catholic, and sex had always involved "pull the nighty down when you are finished" (his words not mine). All sex had ceased when his first wife, Magdalen, developed cancer and died after a long-protracted illness. Within days of moving into his new flat, ladies were knocking on his door with invitations to tea and crumpets. A couple of ladies had made open advances. It was quite clear that nothing was stirring down below, such that he was having to make a hasty retreat. He wondered if anything could be done to help Mr Tinkle (I never cease to be amused by the names men have for the old lady's best friend). I explained to him that his problem was almost certainly related to his previous heart attack and the years of depression associated with his wife's death and subsequent grieving. As there were no signs of life in Mr Tinkle (he even had me going now), the only possibility was an injection for Mr

T, just before planned activity. "Begorrah – you won't be sticking that fecking thing into Mr Tinkle!". I explained how simple the process was, and he presented Mr Tinkle, who had clearly been hibernating below ground level for some time. "Just a tiny prick" I said, regretting my comment almost immediately. "I know" he said, I've needed a mirror to find him for the past 10 years!" Five minutes later, Mr T showed considerable signs of life, but I had learned from my earlier "suck it and see policy" and given 20mcg instead of 10mcg. "Saints be praised" he said, "I'll take 20 of the fecking things, can I use 2 at a time?". I explained that I would recommend the higher dose to guarantee maximum performance, warning him that the erection might last an hour. "Begorrah" he shouted, "Wait until Maud sees this tonight!" I then had to be the bearer of bad news. The NHS in its infinite wisdom allows a maximum of 1 injection per week (more about that later). "To be sure that won't last me until lunchtime tomorrow, I've got Doris for coffee in the morning!"

In the same clinic at around 6pm, I receive a phone call from Ivor Hardy (not his real name), a 92-year-old former golf professional, who was flying out to Antigua the following morning with his considerably younger wife for a 6-week break. He has realised that he was down to his last 4 injections. I explained that, as pharmacy is closed, there was no way that I could get the considerable supply down to London that night. "Damn" he says, "never mind, I'll switch the flight until next Thursday!" Never in their wildest dreams would any GP in the country consider that a 92-year-old man would not even contemplate taking a Caribbean holiday without guaranteed erections.

These 3 cases, along with many others, have convinced me that, as doctors, we have little idea what is important to the lives of our older patients. They could not care in the slightest about their lipids or their eGFR (a test of kidney function) if all is working in the trouser department. This was all made clear by a long-term study of "happiness" from Harvard University in 2018, which showed that "relationships" were number one, well above health and money, in terms of what made people happy. As it is sexual attraction that usually draws us into the most important relationship in our lives, it should surprise nobody of the huge impact of losing that sexual contact and intimacy. In medical school and in hospital practice, I was taught nothing about this. It was only years of really getting to know and understand people in general practice that made me realise that much medical education had little relevance to what was important in people's lives. For many couples, when that physical attraction is lost, there is often little that binds them together. The misery and financial hardships that result from relationship breakups have profound impact, not only on the couple and their children but society in general. If we could only ask questions about sex, especially of men, then we could detect problems, intervene, and save relationships and keep families together. I often comment that I spend most of my time trying to save second and third marriages, as the first had failed long before.

Enough of the serious moralising, back to some more tumescent tales!

It was January 1995, and the clinic was beginning to pick up big time. According to Parkinson's Law, we now, of course, need more staff, so a GP clinical assistant, David Milledge, was appointed for 2 sessions per week to assist in a clinic that nobody knew that we needed 18 months earlier. On 12th, January Cyril Pike, a 75 year- old widower returned. He was yet another senior gent about town. His newly discovered erectile potency was proving a huge hit with the local ladies of Erdington. He currently had 4 different members of the pink rinse brigade in tow and life was getting complicated. With one 72-year-old spinster, Elsie, he was helping her to act out several of her fantasies. He visited her Mondays and Thursdays having carefully administered an injection at least 15 minutes before. Of course, Elsie had no idea of the "magic potion" that Cyril injected that allows him to perform like a 20-year-old stallion. She was just along for the ride, having endured many years of sexual repression with her late husband.

Cyril's role in these fantasies was to knock on the door pretending to be a local tradesman, from window cleaner, to chimney sweep and pool maintenance man, not that Elsie has an open fire, let alone a swimming pool. Cyril looked a sorry soul in the clinic today and Dr Milledge was sitting in on my clinic to learn the secrets of the Sex Tsar. Last Thursday Cyril had duly arrived at Elsie's house at 7.15pm and rang the doorbell, shouting "Gas Man – come to read the meter". Sex in the Gas Man position was Elsie's favourite sexual fantasy, as she always said, "You can stay in all say and nobody comes". This time there was no reply, so Cyril shouted again "Gas Man here", then to his horror he realised that in his excitement, anticipating an evening of endless passion, the old fella was lifeless – he had forgotten to inject himself. He grabbed for the syringe in his pocket and unzipped his overalls – no time to lose. At that moment, Elsie thrust open the front door and wrested Cyril to the ground, "Naughty Mr Gas Man, take me, now," she screamed, clutching at his nether regions. The syringe went flying through the air, spilling all the contents over the carpet. Dr Milledge had been totally silent throughout the consultation but suddenly interrupted "Was it a Shag pile?" "No, an Axminster, I think", replied Cyril. This was a first lesson for Dr M – all humour needs to be pitched at an appropriate level. Clever Dicks are not appreciated in the ED clinic. Alas, for Cyril, that was the end of his relationship with Elsie. His experiences were an eye-opener for Dr Milledge as to the sexual expectations of older men and the voracious demands of older women anxious to make up for lost years.

A commercial preparation of alprostadil had been licensed as Caverject by the aptly named Upjohn Ltd. I was invited to present on "self- injection techniques" at a meeting In Sutton Coldfield in May 1995. I had shopped around for some sort of aid to demonstration and came across a product that seemed to fit the bill. It was called "Grow your own Pecker" and was essentially a small rubber penis that grew to greater than real size when placed in water. On arrival at the meeting, I found that the medic for Upjohn was called Simon Vane Percy and the speaker before me was a Reader in Law at Reading University, called Chris Newdick, who reliably informed me that he lived at 4 Knobcock Lane. The meeting went well, and my inflated pecker stole the show, but unfortunately, I left my pecker in the toilet bag in the hotel room along with my range of expensive toiletries. Two weeks later, I summoned up the courage to ring the hotel to try to recover my bag, hoping that the staff had not opened it to reveal my pecker. I overheard the girl on the phone say to another staff member "It's him!" When I dropped by that evening to collect the bag, it was evident that my pecker had been well handled in those 2 weeks.

The success of the clinic was causing me to question whether we had the appropriate name. Whilst the title "Erectile Dysfunction Clinic" might seem crisp and to the point, I was dealing with many more issues than simply supplying more lead to the pencil. I was keen to be dealing with problems of ejaculation, desire, low testosterone and even problems affecting the female partner and the relationship. Management suggested "Sexual Health Clinic", but to the NHS, Sexual Health means contraception, unplanned pregnancy and STIs, in fact everything to do with having less sex, or indeed, no sex at all. Other names such as "The men's clinic"," Eros", or "Priapus" clinic were simply too pretentious. We decided to stick with ED clinic, with all the limitations.

My youngest son walked in that evening in tears after his teacher had asked them to write a short essay in French about "What their father did for a living". He had been selected to read his essay in class. It began "Il est un docteur du penis". He was given 2 weeks detention

The problem is that the NHS "commissioning system" had made things worse: the patients were now "units" of referral that had to be "costed". In many cases I was seeing a man who might have little wrong with him – apart from being married to the wrong woman. The problem was that the man was the unit of referral and, as such, I have no right to question the partner, let alone offer treatment or advice. This was clear to me when George Dingle first consulted in May 1995. He was 52 and had let himself go, piling on the weight. He had poorly controlled blood pressure and cholesterol, largely because he did not take his tablets. He had been started on injections into the penis and over the course of 6 months and 3 dose increases had reached the maximum dose. This seems strange, so I decided to go back to basics and ask him precisely what was going on in the bedroom. It became quite clear that, once a week he would go to the bathroom, inject himself and venture back into the bedroom expecting his wife, Daphne, to succumb to the majesty of his erection, only to find that she was once again feigning deep insomnia, as she had done for the last 8 years. The reality was that she was no longer remotely interested in "that sort of thing" and whatever "hardening material" I produced would make not a scrap of difference. I suggested that he have a serious "heart to heart" with Daphne, and the look on his face clearly showed that I had hit the nail of the head. I felt certain that he was now going to realise the futility of the last 6 months, only for him to reach the door, turn around and say, "so there's nothing stronger that you can give me!"

Sometimes, of course, the wife may not be the object of the man's fancy. Often, they have a "dancing partner", or they just want to indulge in solo performances just in case an opportunity arises. As Woody Allen famously said, "don't knock masturbation" It's sex with someone I love". One of my favourite websites to recommend is www.masturbation.com which reliably informs us that 95% of men and 89% of women masturbate regularly and explains more than 20 different techniques. In contrast to the old guys, I was seeing many young men with ejaculatory problems. I was becoming increasingly aware that, to some men, ejaculation is an Olympic sport with "personal bests" for categories such as height, distance, volume, and texture. They had little concept that if you can no longer do your PB for the 100 metres or long jump, then your best ejaculatory years might also be behind you.

Although premature ejaculation or PE (much more about that later) is the major problem, many complain about retarded ejaculation or totally impossibility to come. Shane Lingam was 21, a quiet lad seemingly a bit of a geek. He attended with a problem of inability to ejaculate with his new partner, Phoebe, aged 18. The important question to ask is not "if", he masturbated, but "how often?" "Roughly ten times" he answered. He seemed to detect a look of surprise on my face. "Is that too much?" he replied. "Well, ten times per week would be considered above average", was my considered response. "Not weekly" he retorted "I meant daily!". I resisted to temptation to look at my watch and say, "Am I keeping you from something?" My diagnosis here was, of course, *idiosyncratic masturbation*, meaning that the intensity of stimulation required to reach a climax was unlikely to be replicated during vaginal intercourse with his new girlfriend, unless she was a sexual contortionist. We negotiated cessation of masturbation (if possible) to reset the threshold with only once weekly relief being allowed.

I often say that the average UK couple spend more time talking about what colour bathroom suite to buy than they spend discussing their sex lives, yet I have never seen a couple divorce over the colour of their bathroom suite – yet some in avocado must come close. Many men keep their appointments secret from their wives, hoping to "surprise" them, after several years devoid of action. Such a case was Brian Everard, 75, who informed me that his wife was getting desperate, although I noted that she had not attended with him. I duly administered 20mcg of alprostadil and 10 minutes later we had a pretty impressive "lift off". I tried to persuade him that he should wait around for an hour or so to check if things had settled, but he seemed very keen to exit the department, almost as though he had a "fast horse" tied up outside. I recorded Brian as another stunning success for the Tsar and thought nothing more about the case, until 3 weeks later. I was greeted on arrival at the clinic by a gentleman from PALS (Patient Advice and Liaison Services). He had received a letter of formal complaint from a Mrs Ada Everard, who wrote that 3 weeks earlier she had been putting a freshly stuffed chicken in the Aga when her husband Brian, without warning "approached her" from behind "like a wild animal" having just returned from an appointment with Dr Hackett. Luckily my suitably contrite response seemed to do the trick.

As a result of my experiences with Brian and Ada, I decided to rigorously question men as to the level of co-operation with partners. In November 1995, I saw Norman, who reported erectile dysfunction for several years, but on further questioning, it was clear that all his advances to his wife, Ethel had been instantly rejected. Norman was getting regular morning erections. I explained to him that it was pointless to offer him medications and that the problem might not lie with him. Once again, I thought that the Tsar had done an excellent job. Three weeks later the man from PALS was back with a letter of complaint from a Mrs Ethel Dalrymple that her husband, Norman, had returned from a clinic appointment with Dr Hackett, and when she asked what was said, he replied "Dr H said that it's all her fault". The basis for her complaint was that, however clever I was, I knew nothing about her and indeed we had never met. Once again, a suitably humble letter of response seemed to do the trick. I was coming to the conclusion that I just could not win.

In December 1995, as part of the compulsory annual audits, I recorded, over a 1- month period, the percentage of partners accompanying the men in my clinic. This revealed that only 20% of partners attended. On making a robust investigation, I discovered that for the last 2 years, my clinic clerk had been greeting couples by telling the partners "You'll probably have a long wait, and the new coffee shop does an excellent cappuccino and latte, so why don't you pop along there until he's finished". A few words with her and the full audit cycle was completed.

Sometimes attendance with a seemingly devoted partner is not helpful. Cecil and Gladys Wiener attended with problems in the bedroom for several years and the cause was not obvious at first. I note that Gladys seemed to be answering several the questions that would normally require a subjective response from Cecil, such as "do you notice morning stiffness?" Gladys then suddenly revealed "We were referred to you by Professor Kevan Wylie from Sheffield when we recently attended his "small penis clinic". Immediately the elephant in the room revealed itself! During the remainder of the consultation, Cecil's experiences at the "small penis clinic" were mentioned by Gladys 3 more times. My examination of Cecil's genitals duly confirmed that his attendance at the said clinic was entirely appropriate. I offered them some advice, asked them to consider some options and make a follow-up appointment. As I walked past the reception a few minutes later, I overheard Gladys saying to the clinic clerk, in front of a full waiting room "Cecil might not be able to make that date as he has a small penis clinic appointment in Sheffield". I never saw Cyril and Gladys for follow-up.

The following week I received a phone-call from a scientist working for a biopharma company, called Senetek about a new drug in development, called Invicorp. This was also an injection but was reported to be completely painless. They wanted to conduct clinical trials of their new drug and required a UK expert to conduct these. I was acutely conscious that the alprostadil we were using caused intense pain and that we needed something better. The other good news was that Invicorp was reported to carry zero chance of prolonged erection. The drug also came as an auto-injector, perfect for the needle phobic man, which in terms of injecting the penis, applies to most of us. They would be providing the drug for me to use in the clinic and wanted to film the Tsar in action treating patients. I put this to my hospital managers, who were a little sceptical about ethical issues but the offer of a £20k payment soon sorted this. I managed to negotiate that £5K should be allocated for staff attendances at educational meetings – how naïve I was to think that we would ever see this money again!

A week later the camera crew arrived in the department just before a busy clinic. I delivered some words of wisdom to the camera and a couple of patients agreed to have consultations filmed. I had been introduced to a small, shy gentleman who arrived with the Senetek team. His name was Jacob Rosenberg. I was unsure of his role in proceedings. He had said nothing throughout the process, but just as we seem to be closing, he suddenly interjected "I am actually a major investor in the company, I wondered if I might try the injection". I looked quickly over to the product manager, who gave me a nod that clearly indicated that investment from Mr Rosenberg was critical for success. I quickly ascertained that Mr R, who was around 45, had no important medical conditions and was not sexually active. For some reason, I suspected this was probably permanently. I proceeded to inject the lowest dose of Invicorp via the "novel" autoinjector and he verified that the process was completely painless – so far so good. He seemed very impressed when he developed an absolute "stonker" (a term we use regularly in the ED world) within a couple of minutes. I glanced over to the product manager, who gave me the immediate thumbs up, as though the full investment was now in the bag. As we were ending the session, I told Mr R that normally I keep patients in the clinic for at least 90 minutes, but he had a train to catch and business in London that evening and Paris the next day. He reminded me of my recorded interview that listed the post injection problems with this injection as "virtually zero". He glanced at his watch and he and the manager promptly left to catch the train. I was now well behind the clinic and subsequently headed home at 8pm looking forward to a nice glass of Chablis. I was just drifting off in my chair at around 10pm, when the phone rang. It was Mr R, ringing from the Grosvenor Hotel in London. His penis was rock hard and throbbing, but not painful. I suggested that he might like to try some "self-relief" but he had already tried this 4 times and the erection kept coming back. I advised him that the lack of pain was reassuring that that there were no recorded cases of priapism with Invicorp. He seemed relieved. I got up early the next morning for a full day of general practice, and reached home about 9pm, hoping my dinner would not be too spoilt. I had barely started when the phone rang. A lady with a strong French accent announced that this was the Ritz in Paris and she was putting me through to Mr Rosenberg in room 101. He could barely speak "I think it's on fire" he mumbled. I asked some of my standard questions on erection hardness and we agreed that "Yes, he could probably use it to bang in a 3-inch nail". He had called off his business meeting and sought the help of the duty manager at the Ritz. Being French, he seemed to have a novel suggestion that none of us in the UK would have considered. He rang a lady who often helped discerning clients of the Ritz in need of relief. Two hours later she had left, apparently requesting twice her normal call out fee. There was no alternative but to give him the emergency phone number of a top French Urologist I knew, Professor Stephane Droupy (I jest not). I heard nothing further from Mr R, but I am sure that he will always remember his impulse suggestion to "give it a go". He clearly had a night in Paris that he will never forget. I bumped into Professor Droupy at a meeting a couple of months later and he had no recollection of Mr R, so I was uncertain as to whether I should record him as the first priapism with Invicorp or simply an innocent Jewish gentleman who could tell an interesting tumescent tale of 2 cities.

My documentary for Senetek led to a couple of clinical trials and lecture trips to San Francisco and Kuala Lumpur in the summer of 1996. I was becoming an international Sex Tsar, but things were about to get even better. In early March 1996, I had a call a call from a Dr Ian Osterloh of Pfizer UK, that an oral drug was being developed to treat ED and I had been selected as a possible centre to carry out research. As I had witnessed the way NHS hospitals approach research which essentially consisted of "You do the work and we'll take the money" along with the disappearance of the £5K allocated for doctor education, I developed a different approach. I had developed a small clinic in a barn conversion adjacent to my home specially for clinical trials avoiding much of the red tape involved in the

NHS. In early June 1996, Dr Osterloh attended with Professor Alan Riley to explain the first UK clinical trial of a drug called sildenafil. I was aware that a couple of oral drugs had been tested and failed miserably so I was dubious to hear of a drug developed to treat blood pressure and heart disease. The interesting fact was that the patients had refused to return to tablets at the end of the study. After the meeting, I remember going back to Sally and saying, "I've just met a couple of wackos who think they have a drug to give you an erection"; how wrong I was! Much more of this in later chapters.

CHAPTER 2.
Earlier Education and Medical School Years

In June 1968 as a rather "young" 17-year-old, I arrived at Kings College Hospital Medical School, in leafy Camberwell, for interview. I had been "groomed" (a term with a different meaning then) for a place at Cambridge but my parents had split up and I was made to board from the age of 16. A further year of boarding, with 9pm bedtimes was something I desperately needed to escape, but more about that later.

Thankfully in those days Medical School interviews were somewhat different. I remember 3 rather elderly men, all with waistcoats and half-spectacles. To my surprise, the one on the left produced a rugby ball and threw is at me. I managed to catch it at the second attempt. He mumbled "clearly not a fly-half". I explained that the heights of my "rugger" achievement was second team centre for Queen Elizabeth Grammar School, Wakefield and I was more a "round ball man". I then realised that the top sheet of paper in front of him was a set of rugby positions and his major duty was to improve Kings' chances in next year's hospitals cup. Suddenly a cricket ball flew at me from the hand of the consultant on the left. I took a fine single-handed catch and his eyes lit up. His questions revealed that I was first XI batsman for the last 2 years and currently top of the batting averages. "Opener I hope" he said as he made notes on his sheet. The gent in the middle had spotted that I have played a lot of chess in British Championships (boring I know) and mentioned the name of a very senior player that I had recently beaten. Without thinking, I answered "He used to be very good, but he is long past his best". I realised that I should have considered my answer for longer as he retorts "He is my younger brother!" That was the sum of questions asked at my interview – an offer of 3 Ds appeared in the post. How things have changed.

My early education had been very haphazard. My father had been an Australian spitfire pilot and married my mother aged, 17, immediately after the war and then relocating back to Townsville in North Queensland. He was something of a "hero" having been shot down over Northern Italy and escaped with the help of the Italian resistance. As he died in 2013, aged 93, he was the last surviving Australian Spitfire pilot. They went to great lengths to locate him, sending a deputation to the UK to persuade him to return for Anzac Day in 2012, but he was too frail. We were glad to be able to look after him in an adjoining "granny flat" in his later years. For those remotely interested, his story can be found by searching on "Jack Hackett – Australian spitfire pilot". Be careful not to get the alcoholic priest, father Jack Hackett of Father Ted fame, although there were some similarities in later life.

My mother, Moyra, must have been the ultimate "whingeing pom", such that, after one futile effort to return to the UK in 1955, one of the coldest winters on record, we eventually returned for good in 1960. Despite going to 11 different schools by the age of 11, I was fortunate to be just young enough to take the 11 plus and obtain a scholarship to Queen Elizabeth Grammar school Wakefield. The most famous old boy was John George Hague, the acid bath murderer, notorious for dissolving at least 6 bodies (he claimed 9) in acid. He won the school chemistry prize as well as the Provost of Wakefield Divinity prize. He was executed on 10th August 1949.

I searched for clues in my family history that I was destined for a career as a Sex Tsar but found little evidence. My father was contacted from our Australian family that a distant relative was general Sir John Winthrop Hackett, a distinguished commander in the Normandy landings, who was, by chance Principal of Kings College from 1968 to 1975, the very time I had applied to Kings. My father wrote to him to point out my application for a place at Kings, only to receive a response that could be summarised in two words.

Further research showed that Sir John's father, Sir Winthrop Hackett had been a prominent politician in Western Australian and Chancellor of the University of Perth, with several streets and landmarks named after him. On visiting Perth in 2000, I discovered a copy of the Western Australian Newspaper rating him, most impressively, the "Fifteenth most influential Western Australian of all time". On my return to Perth in 2014, I discovered that he had been elevated to 14th, following the conviction of Rolf Harris. There were rumours that a great uncle had disgraced the family by being court-marshalled in 1912 for having sex with a suffragette, which seemed extremely harsh, until I later learned that she was chained to the railings of 10 Downing Street at the time.

Throughout my school career, I remember that I always intended to do medicine, until I had good "O" level results in Latin and the Headmaster, Mr J.K Dudley, identified me as a potential classics scholar. My father gave him short shift at the next parents evening by telling him in blunt Aussie fashion that no son of his was doing "poofta" subjects. This was typical of Dad, who was once reprimanded for telling his secretary that a recent company reshuffle made him feel" like a shag on a rock", expressing feelings of professional isolation rather than sexual preference. I remember being "fast streamed" along with 2 other students, Michael Viner, and David Luesley who both went on to eminence as Professors of Obstetrics and Gynaecology, whilst my career pathway was less certain.

I probably played too much sport, especially cricket. My "rugger" career faltered when my mother was concerned that my lack of pace was detected very early and I was forced to play in the second row, resulting in some painful injuries. Fearful that I might be developing cauliflower ears, my mother knitted me a white fur-fabric scrum cap, insisting that I wore it for the next match. At age 14, the laughter in the changing room on the first day I wore the scrum cap remains in my memory as perhaps the most humiliating day of adolescence. I started playing football (the round ball game) for a local team but was spotted by a school master and reported to Mr J K Dudley. I was summoned to his office and recall him looking over his spectacles. "Now Geoffrey, you have reached an important stage in your development". I remember this was his opening gambit in all circumstances. "You have been observed playing...", a palpable lump came to his throat as he read the words off his notes "...Association football". "Correct me if I am wrong but I understand that you did intend to go to University..." I got the point and was back in the third team rugby the next week, minus my bespoke scrum cap.

I remember getting into the school cricket team at 15, and my 3rd match was against our biggest rivals, Nottingham High School, who gave us a hiding most years. I recall that before the match on July 30th, 1966 (an important date), the senior players made a bet that we would all pay £1 each to anyone who made either 50 or 5 wickets against them. Nottingham compiled a big score and we were soon in trouble. I dug in for perhaps the most boring 52 on record, in 3 hours, but worst of all it meant that I kept all 22 players, plus umpires, away from watching any of the World Cup final. Needless to say, that all bets were off because of the mind-numbing boredom of my performance.

At age 16, my parents went through a "difficult phase" and I had to complete my education as a boarder, meaning bedtime at 9pm with Mr Dudley supervising "lights out". Usually as he left the dormitory, he would say "Shufflebotham, whatever you're doing under the covers, stop it now!" I always wondered what happened to Shufflebotham. There was nothing that JKD liked more than a spot of impromptu umpiring when he turned up to a cricket match. On one occasion this involved bringing one of my rare free-flowing innings to a swift conclusion with a truly shocking LBW decision. My understandable disappointment and reaction led to another appearance in his office the next day. "Now Geoffrey, you have reached an important stage in your development" followed by another of his frequent missives "You can always tell the character of a man by the way he plays his cricket". I decided that there was no alternative but to play everything with a straight bat from then on.

I would have to say that the lack of outside distraction and being tucked up in bed by 9pm at age 16-17 did help the exam performance and kept me out of trouble, certainly when it came to any problems with the opposite sex. I therefore decided that I could not contemplate another year of sexual repression and early nights listening to Shufflebotham's slapping noises under the sheets, so the medical school applications went in a year early.

I was a regular attender at Catholic church, and in retrospect a bit of a "goody two shoes". I was proud never to receive a "bad record" during my school days. I attended confession regularly with Father Kelly and often struggled to find any bad things that I had done, apart from disputing LBW decisions. I usually threw in a confession of "impure thoughts on 2 occasions", as this was good for 3 Our Fathers and 3 Hail Mary's maximum, not too time consuming. Father Kelly's response was always the same, "Might these impure thoughts involve fornication of the flesh?" He was clearly keen to get specific details. Although I was never quite sure at that stage what he was getting at, I denied all such activity as I am sure that the penance would have been much more severe.

Following my demanding medical school interviews at Kings, I managed to achieve the required grades and arrived at Kings College Hall of residence (fondly known as Plats) in Denmark Hill on 30th September 1968.

For the first 3 weeks, I actually believed that the doors of Plats closed at 11pm, until I looked out my first- floor window and saw at least 5 girls coming in through ground floor windows. The days were spent commuting on the train from Denmark Hill to Blackfriars and the walk along to Kings College in the Strand. Most of this period remains a blur apart from the stench of the Anatomy dissection room. I remember that our cadaver was a sailor with a very large dick. Unfortunately, the future Sex Tsar did not even get a look in, as Hilary, one of the students in my group, took control of the genital dissection. The aroma in the Chesham, where we had lunch, was marginally better as it was beans and chips with everything. I remember several great concerts, with the Who, the Move and Emerson Lake and Palmer. I played football and cricket whenever I could, hoping to repay the trust placed in me at my interviewers. I was definitely not mixing with the academic high- fliers at this stage. I think I was a late developer.

Having learned that it was possible to smuggle girls into Plats, my big opportunity seemed to have arrived after a dance at St Gabriel's teacher training college, but I had not reckoned with a couple of mates, who should probably remain nameless in view of their highly successful careers (especially in law and the church). Let us call them Tom and Jon. As I opened the door to go straight for my Leonard Cohen (seduction special) album. I noted that not only was my room rather chilly, it was virtually empty. A glance out of the open window revealed my bed and desk hanging over the side of the building, suspended by knotted sheets – I had fallen in with dangerous people. From that day on I kept all cards close to my chest.

On my long summer holiday, I took a job driving a van around the North west, delivering dog food to pet shops. On my second day I was delivering to a shop in Toxteth and was invited in for a coffee and cake by the owner. Ten minutes later I came out to find that, not only had the stock been taken from the van but the wheels were missing as well. This remains the only time in my life that I have been fired. I have had a healthy distrust of Scousers from that date.

These were great years to be in London but for me the social life. In 1969, we had bands like Thin Lizzy and the Moody Blues appearing at Plats and nearby Goldsmiths College. I can remember chatting with Phil Lynott at the bar, not knowing how big the band would become. Unfortunately, like many rock legends, he died young. We even had Queen appear as a support band at the medical school in 1970. The main act was Gary Wright's Wonder Wheel, who have not lived long in the memory of readers. Normally nobody left the bar to watch the support, but I can remember trying to get some mates out telling them that the support band sounded pretty good, but the lead singer was a bit weird.

Having coasted my way through school, I do not think I really appreciated that now I was in an elite environment where hard work was essential. I failed my anatomy, not that I could blame Hilary's dominance of the genital dissection, as I missed several sessions. It was the first exam that I ever failed, and it was a shock. It meant that I missed the summer holiday to have to redo all the subject. I had been set back several months.

Luckily, I squeezed through the exams second time and it was off to the hospital. Tom and Jon had come down a few days earlier to find a suitable flat in the Camberwell/Herne Hill area. I arrived at the Medical School prior to making my way up to the flat. I heard some laughing at the next table as it seems that some "morons" had actually rented a rat- infested hole that had been empty for over a year. The address of 74 Elfindale Rd, Herne Hill, sounded vaguely familiar. I reached into my pocket and took out the paper "No – I was one of the morons!". The reality was even worse than expected, especially as I had last choice of bedroom- and yes, the rats were huge. I remember nights where there were more than one of them running across the sheets. Luckily for Tom and Jon, they spent most time at various girlfriends' pads. Unfortunately, student flats in Herne Hill were under local mafia control and good ones only came up occasionally. Three months later, I was able to move to a much better flat on the first floor in Herne Hill, at £2.20p per week. I shared a bedroom with another medic, Ed Morris, and his kestrel, which spent the night attached to the end of his bed (the kestrel, not Ed). I remember nights when I woke with the moonlight streaming through the windows and these huge flapping wings, like something from an Edgar Alan Poe novel. One of my flatmates, Paul Dubbins was an excellent cook and went on to be a highly successful Radiologist in Plymouth, where he later worked with Dr Bollinger. Things had really taken a turn for the better. My day for cooking was Thursday and it was always Shepherd's pie. Many who know me well might comment that little progress has been made in the many years that followed.

I started at Kings on Mr Leonard Cotton's (LC) surgical firm, and this was to be my first house job 3 years later. My lasting recollection involved Dr Graham Jackson, later to be one of our finest cardiologists. LC had very bad psoriasis as was evident in theatre and must have been an infection risk, but nobody was brave enough to say anything. I remember when we were 3-deep in theatre watching a femoral artery graft. LC had painstaking prepared the graft and was just about to suture it in into place. This was the key moment of the operation. As house surgeon, GJ was in control of suction. Unfortunately, he leaned forward at the crucial moment and sucked the entire graft up the tube and into the waste bottle. LC, with a ruddy complexion at the best of times, looked as though he was going to explode, his eyes about to pop out on stalks. "Get out, Jackson" he said, and Graham skulked off towards the locker room. This might have been Graham's lowest moment. It was 38 year later that I summoned up the courage to remind him that I was there on that fateful day.

There was always the odd precocious student who was out to impress, but this never worked on Mr Hedley Berry. One student, Pringle (not his real name), was being particularly objectionable, asking questions when he already knew the answers. I could see HB getting more exasperated. At a crucial stage, HB asked him if he could see the large cyst on the liver and urged him forward to get a better view. At the critical point, I watched him stick a scalpel in the cyst and bang, the bloody fluid went straight into the student's right eye. Pringle immediately rubbed his eye. Mr Berry immediately announced "Pringle, you're no longer sterile, you will have to leave the theatre!" Afterwards he announced, "Thank god for that, some peace at last, how does everybody rate our chances for the winter Ashes series down under?"

Moving onto my medical firm on the Liver Unit, it was quite clear that my future was more likely to lie in Medicine that in Surgery. Dr Roger Williams had been appointed in charge of the unit in 1966 and Liver transplants began in 1968 and it is incredible that he remains clinically active in 2020 at age 89. It was strange working in a specialist unit where every third patient had Crigler Najjar Syndrome or Wilson's disease, when I never saw a case of either in the next 40 years.

I remember on my third week on the firm, being asked by the house officer to put up a drip on a patient with jaundice on the male medical ward. I was very flattered that he chose me, as I always thought that I had a good touch at getting into veins. I spotted this bright yellow chap at the end of the ward. He seemed surprised that he was having a drip, but I had been warned that he was slightly confused, so I pushed on. It went very well, and I was quite chuffed until the nurse pulled back the curtains around the next bed, to reveal a chap who was an even deeper yellow. "The medical student will be along to set up your drip, soon Mr Warboys" said the nurse. I felt a sinking feeling in the pit of my stomach. Retiring to the clinical room, I prepared another trolley and tiptoed down the ward to Mr

Warboys, closing the curtains behind. Of course, his veins were dreadful, and it took me 5 goes to get the drip sited. As I closed the curtains, I noticed that the patient next door had drifted off to sleep. I quietly sneaked in and removed the free-flowing drip without waking him. None of the nurses noticed a thing and when he woke, he probably thought he had dreamt the whole thing. After this, I understood why they painstakingly check the names and wristbands on patients.

We then moved on to “special firms”, such as ENT, Eyes, Psychiatry, Orthopaedics etc, which consisted mainly of boring outpatient attendances. This provided a great opportunity to maximise cricket to 3 times per week. One of our group suffered “burnout” and escaped to Tibet for 6 months to find his inner self through meditation. Having found it, he returned to Kings, intending to beg his way back onto the course, only to find that he had a full set of high marks for all these specialities. He later realised that he was fortunate to bear a very close resemblance to one of the smartest guys in the year.

I remember that my Psychiatry firm was interrupted when one of the consultants was arrested for undressing the stripper on-stage at the Skinners Arms in Kennington. Some firms did involve evenings and nights on call. Sleeping over in the student accommodation in Bessemer Rd, next to the hospital allowed me to reacquaint myself with the joys of sharing a bed with vermin. My special recollection of Orthopaedics was a heavy drinking Welsh registrar who performed excellent surgery, but only after 10pm and 7 pints when his tremor had settled. The problem was that he expected the house officers and students to match him drink for drink all evening in the bar. Alcohol was everywhere in hospitals in those days. How things have changed in an age of zero tolerance nowadays. There was a mystical society at Kings, termed “the Newts”, that involved drinking 7 pints in 1 hour without pissing or puking. To my eternal shame, I failed the initiation ceremony twice.

I remember going on the coach to Chislehurst to support Kings on a hospital cup rugby match v Guys. We narrowly lost but were just getting on to the coach when a Guys supporter in a striped blazer with a bottle of celebratory “Champers” still in his hand, asked if he could grab a ride on our coach as their “chaps” had left. It was clear after a few minutes on the coach that his pompous gloating was not going down well. The net result was that his clothes were jettisoned along the A2, and he was eventually ejected totally naked in front of a packed bus shelter in rush hour outside the Maudsley Hospital. I understand that he was reviewed by psychiatrists in casualty and narrowly avoided admission under a section.

My second- year clinical studies concluded with Obstetrics and Gynaecology, by far the most interesting part of my medical education. It was 3rd June 1972 and the first gynaecology ward round. I had been warned that this consultant had a “party trick” for new students. This involved stressing the vital importance of traditional skills such as urine testing, including “tasting”, the urine in an emergency. He demonstrated this by dipping his index finger in the urine and then putting the finger in his mouth, and after considering the impact on his palate, he would announce, “a trace of sugar and moderate protein”. Only those of us with a keen eye, spotted that he was really testing our powers of observation as he would dip his index finger in the urine but lick his middle finger! He invited a female student to verify his findings. She cautiously moved towards the sample, dipped her index finger, and put it in her mouth, visibly shaking. She began to gag and splutter and had to withdraw from the round. A smug smile came to the consultant's face, as he turned to me and said, "Hackett, what about you, care to check my findings?" I confidently stepped forward, put my index finger in the urine and sucked long and thoughtfully on my middle finger. "Mmm, definite sugar, a trace of ketones, I suspect that she is taking garlic and magnesium supplements and is 8 weeks pregnant". His smug smile changed to a scowl as he realised that his party trick had been exposed by a young clever dick.

It was June 1972 and I was in theatre at Dulwich Hospital with 5 other students, leaning forward to watch Sir Basil S, who must have been in his mid-70s, perform a hysterectomy for fibroids. It was clear as students that the Senior Registrar (SR) was really in charge. "I'll get that bleeder", Sir Basil would say, as he surged forward with the cautery, only for the SR to casually stop the bleeding. As they came to the stage of removing the uterus, the size of a football, Sir Basil insisted on performing this stage personally whilst the SR divided the last few adhesions. At the critical point that the uterus became free, it slipped from his grasp and went flying across the room. As a predatory centre forward, who fancied himself as good in the air, seeing this football size sphere flying past at head height, I felt an irresistible urge to attempt a flying header but luckily missed, as the uterus hit the far wall and bounced several times around the theatre. "I think it's out", the SR casually announced. "Good", said Sir B, I think I can now leave you to close, and made his way to the changing room for a well -earned rest. This experience showed me 2 things. Even at that stage, that surgery is a young man's game, and that my finishing skills were already blunted in 6 weeks without a game. In retrospect, the weight of the muscular sphere on my head would probably have rendered me unconscious, causing me to worry about the cumulative damage I may have done to my brain with repeated heading. Still I see no sign of losing my mental edge, although readers of this book may disagree.

" I think it's finally out, Sir Basil"

It was 3rd July 1972, and I was attending my first gynae outpatient clinic on a 1:1 basis with the SR. We were in a steaming hot and sweaty community clinic, in deepest Brixton, long before the days of air-conditioning. The first patient was an amply proportioned Jamaican lady, Mrs Mariposa Clarke, aged 40, who was already placed up in stirrups with legs spread wide apart. After the SR had completed his vaginal examination, he turned to me and said, "Now Hackett, your turn for examination. Please describe your findings". Already I had learned that the wrong thing to do was just charge in, so I politely asked, "Mrs Clarke, do you mind if I examine you? Please let me know if you experience any discomfort". I grabbed an extra-large glove that stretched well up the forearm. I heard a cautious "OK" from further up the couch, so continued. Mr Green, the SR, sensed my uncertainty and began guiding me through. "First of all, spread the labia and inspect the perineum, clitoris and urethra for signs of atrophy or inflammation. Next, describe the general texture and muscle tone of the vagina, then assess whether the cervix is smooth." In Mrs Clarke's case the cervix was a long way in, but, after 30 seconds, I found it and reported it felt normal. "Now, sweep your hand into the left fornix, palpate the left fallopian tube, and seek out the left ovary, can you feel it?". By now, I was in up to my right elbow. "Good, now slip your left hand up on the abdomen and palpate the uterus for size and irregularity and sweep your hand around the back to the cervix to palpate the Pouch of Douglas, posteriorly. Is everything normal?". By now I was in above the right elbow and at full stretch, "I think so?". "Now sweep into the right fornix. This will be more difficult, as you are right-handed, but I want you to pay special attention to the right tube and ovary and tell me what you find". He was now giving me a strong clue that I should find something abnormal at this stage, so I made sure that I was feeling this area very carefully. This took several minutes. Suddenly, with no warning, I began to feel intense squeezing pressure on my right hand, extending up my arm and becoming slightly uncomfortable. This continued for about 20 seconds and they slowly subsided. I then heard a long groan from further up the couch and after a further few seconds, Mrs Clarke announced, "Man, you just rang my chimes!"

After the Gynae firm, the focus shifted to Obstetrics, which most medical students probably remember as the most enjoyable part of training. Because London teaching hospitals are highly specialised, students are sent far and wide to get hands on experience and clock up their required number of deliveries. I was sent to Odstock Hospital in Salisbury, which at this time consisted of World War II prefabricated buildings, a complete change from Kings. The intensive 24-hour life of the Maternity unit there was a wonderful experience for 6 weeks, but I still managed to get back for the early matches of the new football season, a 200-mile round trip. I was later presented a trophy for playing more games of football and scoring more goals than any other player. I also captained the cricket team to 2 university cups. I reflected that I did not waste my time at medical school completely.

I returned to London reflecting that I had just spent 3 months dealing with the sexual and reproductive aspects of the female. I had received virtually no training whatsoever on the male reproductive system. At this stage, even urology was merely a sub-section of general surgery. Little has changed in medical education over the intervening 47 years.

We were now moving into our fifth- year and building to our final exams. At this stage, we had the opportunity to travel on our externship to gain valuable experience. Most altruistic students opted for third world countries in Africa, but those of us with debts could opt for the United States. I chose Grant

Hospital, Columbus, Ohio, for 3 months and set out in November on 19th November 1972. It was one of their worst winters on record with thick snow when I arrived and even thicker when I left the following February. The good news is that we were paid for doing the medical assessments of patients on admission. Every morning, there was a scrum, with 5 New Zealand students, to get access to the patients as soon as possible. This was great experience to sharpen up my skills, but it was all full on with clinical meetings throughout the day. Luckily, the social life in the evenings made up for everything.

My lasting recollection was Christmas Day 1972, when I received invitation from 3 different consultants to Christmas dinner, as I it would have been rude to turn any down. It worked out that, due to different mealtimes, I could get to all 3. I decided not to drink alcohol at the first 2 in order to avoid detection and then cut loose at the third. I arrived at the third consultant's house absolutely stuffed but looking forward to a few beers as I had a taxi booked to get back to the hospital. The sight of the largest turkey I had ever seen, and the sight of many children should have given me a clue. I was offered a glass of pomegranate juice, with the explanation that they trusted that I was aware that they were Mormons!

On January 20th, 1973, I went with the New Zealanders to Richard Nixon's second inauguration celebrations in Washington, little realising the furore that was soon to break. Two weeks later it was back home and the run in to finals. By this time, and with the US externship, I had lost contact with my old friends and made the wise decision to return to Plats to ensure that I got down to work and did not blow it this time. I was immediately struck with how young the new students looked. Some would come and sit next to me at meals, hoping to make a new friend. They soon realised that I was not there to make some "fresher friends". Luckily, second time round I did manage to get down to work, the final few revision firms and, of course, even more cricket and football. I duly passing my finals in late 1973. The great thing about medical qualification is that we all tended to just pass or fail, with very few achieving honours. Now I was a proper doctor and good to go.

CHAPTER 3.

This Really Did Hurt – Junior Hospital Doctor Years

It was January 1974, and the results were in. The good thing about Medicine is that you either pass or fail and very few ever get "honours", certainly never when you played as much cricket and football as I did. I was about to learn that all that effort had not been wasted. The first house officer jobs were up on the Medical School notice board. To the complete surprise of everybody, I had got the plumb house surgeon job working for Mr Leonard Cotton and Mr Hedley Berry. I would quickly point out that this was not remotely related to any surgical skill displayed in my training but purely down to the many hours of monotonously nurdling singles to fine leg over the last 4 years. It so happened that Hedley Berry was the greatest fan of Geoffrey Boycott and had always embraced everything that was fine about Yorkshire cricket. He was president of the Kings College Cricket and Football Clubs and had spent many hours watching me compile some of the slowest 50s in hospital cricket history. He was also a life-long Leeds United fan and clearly spotted a bit of Alan "sniffer "Clarke in my predatory finishing. The list had only been up for a day before a formal complaint had been lodged by a female honours graduate. In a measured response, Mr Berry commented that "If he were to be stuck in theatre with a house surgeon for 5 hours, then it would be much more tolerable to be able to discuss whether Geoff Boycott's mother could really have tamed the Indian pace attack with a stick of rhubarb or why Leeds United were the finest team English football had ever produced". He also observed that "anybody who could get 11 lazy medical students to play cricket twice a week could certainly organise his operating list". To me this was a complete vindication of the medical interview process 5 years earlier. Although, in the words of JK Dudley, you could tell that Hedley Berry was a fine man by the way he played his cricket, there would be no place for his approach in modern day human resources.

House Surgeon (Jan-June 1974)

I remember my first day as a house-surgeon at Kings. The job was supposed to be 1 in 2, which means that you worked until about 7pm every day and on alternate nights and weekends you worked right though. This seemed bad enough until I was greeted by Mr Cotton on my first day. He informed me that he liked to do a ward round each evening and every weekend, and he expected me to be there: no such thing as overtime then. Tell that to the youngsters today and they do not believe you!

The major task of a house surgeon is to make sure that operating lists run smoothly. This involved "clerking" the patients by taking a history and sorting out their investigations, medication, and blood tests pre-operatively. Most importantly, for a vascular surgeon, cross matching several units of blood for the following day was crucial. Unfortunately for me, on week 2 of my job, there was a national blood shortage. I received a phone-call at 7am on the day to tell me that no blood was available for the major procedure. On my arrival in theatre, the anaesthetist was sympathetic and left very quickly "mmm, I think I will leave it to you to tell your boss!". To this day I can remember watching Mr Cotton walk the entire length of the hospital corridor only to have to break the news to him. There was a pause of a few seconds, the blood surged into his neck veins and what followed was the closest I have seen to the Incredible Hulk metamorphosis. I cannot remember his parting words as he turned and departed, but “imbecile” was somewhere in there. I realised that it was going to be very difficult to come back from this... but on my first weekend on call things were about to get worse.

It was around midnight on Saturday when my bleep went after a very demanding day on duty following on from a chaotic first week. It was a call from the private wing. It was a surprise to me that we had a private wing, let alone that I was on-call for Mr Cotton’s patients there.

I arrived on the ward to be summoned to the bed of a gentleman from Saudi Arabia who spoke no English. It was clear that he was in considerable pain in his foot and lower leg and was getting no relief from his post-operative pethidine injections. A review of the operation notes from the Friday told me that Mr Cotton had performed a femoral angioplasty, a graft to bypass a blocked artery. What we now know is that this was not a very good procedure as these grafts frequently became blocked and clearly little or no blood was getting to this man’s foot. He was heading towards gangrene with probable loss of his leg. It was now 2am and there was no alternative but to ring Mr Cotton at home. I took several deep breaths and dialled the number. After around 10 rings, I heard the gruff tones for Mr C and started to tell him the story. To my surprise he simply slammed the phone down on me. At this moment I felt very lonely and isolated. I simply could not face ringing him again, especially if my judgement was wrong. I noted from the records that the anaesthetist for this man's operation, Dr H, was the same one who showed me sympathy a few days earlier. At 2.30 am I rang Dr H and he agreed with me and contacted Mr C. The result was that the patient was back in surgery by 5am. I looked in the next day and the man's foot was looking "less blue" but I feared the longer-term outlook for his leg was not good. The next week in theatre, Dr H smiled at me and remarked, "Well done young man, that took balls!" I received no comment from Mr C. This use of house surgeons to cover consultant's private patients as part of the NHS contract would not be allowed today.

Effectively, this job was virtually on-call 100% of the time, most often with the same SR, Mr Charles Derry. I remember one crazy night on 13th March 1974 when we were struggling to deal with massive arterial blood loss and things were clearly going rapidly down-hill. Emergency blood was being sent from the transfusion centre and, at 3am, I was sent to find out what was happening. As I entered the main corridor, I saw a uniformed courier sprinting down the corridor with a large box. He tripped and went flying through a glass door. As he fell the blood box went flying and, as he stretched his hand to break his fall, he severed his brachial artery on the glass. The spurting arterial blood hit the ceiling. Within seconds, it was like a scene from Reservoir Dogs. I had to compress the brachial artery and shout for help. We had to abandon the case in theatre to deal with the courier, who was rapidly bleeding to death. Of course, we had to send for several units of O negative blood as the samples he brought were incompatible.

On 15th March 1974, it was another busy weekend and I was admitting another patient in casualty. I looked across at the duty board and the 3 surgical house-officers for the weekend and the choices for the patients were Drs Hackett, Cutting or Carver, a gruesome combination. I was admitting a Mr Sylvester Brown, 42, from Trinidad, who had an indoor TV aerial rammed up his arse. In those days, TV aerials consisted of 2 long pointed prongs and we all spent many hours wandering around the house only to discover that the only decent picture was achieved by hanging out of the window. He claimed to have been watching his favourite programme, "Till death us do part", in the nude at home when he slipped, accidentally sitting on the coffee table where he had placed the aerial for best reception. He was in some distress and it was clear that he had perforated bowel and bladder, at least. His cover was blown when his hysterical wife, Princess, arrived later and proceeded to list the other various objects that she would shove up the next time he came home early and caught him on the job with the slag from his office. This poor chap had extensive internal damage and his case became the subject of a major paper in the Lancet.

"Perfect picture, you've just rammed the aerial up my arse."

Patients in Accident and Emergency were assessed in bays divided by curtains, and in cubicle 1, David Cutting, still a mate today, was clerking in a deaf 82-year-old, Doris, with abdominal pain. She was accompanied by her older and I suspect, deafer, husband. David was having to shout at the top of his voice, and, as usual, when patients do not understand, we shout even louder. "Where is the pain?", "Eh" she replied. "Is it Down here?" "Oh... yes". "Is it sharp... or dull?" "Eh", "IS IT SHARP OR DULL?" "Sharp, I think". It continued like this, and by now, everybody in the department was hanging on every word. After about 5 minutes, he turned to the husband in frustration. "Any previous operations?" "Gall bladder 1965" the old man answered. There was almost palpable relief from David as he was now making progress at last. He piled on with his questions for a further 10 minutes, writing hastily in the notes. “Waterworks problems?” “No”. “What age did the periods stop?”, asked David. There was a sudden hesitation in the flow, “Oh, are you asking about the wife?”. A sound of head banging on the wall followed by the ripping of several sheets of paper. As David pulled back the curtains, he was greeted by a standing ovation.

I always prided myself on being a good communicator with patients. It was 17th March 1974, and Horace Potter had come in for a vascular bypass operation the next day. He had severely blocked arteries in the left leg. Having taken his history, I proceeded to draw detailed diagrams of his legs, explaining where the blockages were and how we would bi-pass these obstructions. I explained about dressings and drains, pain relief and how long he would be in hospital.” Do you have any further questions, anything at all?”, I asked? “No, I don’t think so”, was his reply. As I returned to the desk in the middle of the ward to write up the notes, I saw his visitors arrive. His wife asked, “Hello Horace, what is it that they are doing to you tomorrow?” “Not a clue”, he replied, “Nobody tells you a bloody thing around here”.

I know that he must have done well, as 2 years later, as a medical registrar, I found a group of nurses laughing at drawings of a legs of a Mr Horace Potter in a set of notes. They were struggling to read the doctor’s signature. I confess that I never owned up to those drawings. I may be a good communicator, but I have always had the artistic and handwriting skills of a 4-year-old. Most doctors have realised that illegible handwriting can often be a major advantage.

One of the important roles of a house surgeon was to arrange a second opinion from another specialist. On 21st March 1994, I had been asked to seek a cardiology opinion on an 80-year-old gentleman as to whether he was fit for surgery. I duly lodged to request with the cardiology secretary. Two days later, on the routine ward round, we arrived at the bed, and introduced Mr Berry, my boss, to the patient and gently shook him to wake him from sleep. We could get no response as he had clearly passed away. We pulled to curtains and I took his notes to the nursing station to make an entry. I noted that the cardiologist had been to see him 1 hour earlier and made the entry, "There is nothing that I can offer this man, he is dead!" I can only assume that he must have been in a hurry.

One of the interesting hospital characters in those days was Peter Mayhew, alias "Peter the Porter", who was 7ft 3inches tall and suffered from Marfan's Syndrome, a condition associated with giant stature and heart valve problems. He usually worked with another porter who was little over 5 foot and they were usually on duty for the mortuary. They were quite a sinister pair. We were stunned when Peter announced one day that he was leaving the bright lights of Camberwell for a career in Hollywood. He went on to play Chewbacca in the Star Wars films until his death in 2019, aged 74.

I often think back to the surgical wards in the seventies. In those days, patients would remain on the ward for 7-10 days after an appendicectomy, gall bladder removal or hernia repair, procedures that nowadays are day cases or overnight stays. We used to conduct ward rounds on patients who were essentially just on prolonged bed rest. We even had convalescent homes in the country where patients could enjoy the fresh mountain air as they recovered. How things have changed.

As penalty for a top surgical job, house officers were usually to be sent to some god forsaken place for Medical placement. In my case it was Isle of Thanet Hospital in Ramsgate in late 1974, working for consultants, Drs Lillicrap and Cocking (I jest not). This job was full on with virtually no time off and only 2 games of cricket in the 6 months. Almost every day there were no empty beds and I vividly remember a visit from Princess Anne. This involved several weeks of intense preparation, as nothing very exciting ever happened in Ramsgate. As the tour progressed, we were moving beds through corridors and back into the wards that she had just left, to prevent her seeing the chaos. The manoeuvre was conducted with military precision.

By now, I was still not certain where I was going in my career, but has ruled out surgery, in favour of medicine. I applied for a 2-year medical registrar rotation back at Kings, but although unsuccessful, I was offered a guaranteed post 6 months later. I accepted as it would give me some stability rather than moving around ever six months. With a medical Registrar job sorted, I decided to take a convenient 6-month post registration house officer job in Gynaecology back at Dulwich Hospital, part of the Kings group. This was a decision that was viewed later as being indecisive and subsequently worked against me.

The Gynae job for Mr John Studd was tough, with around 15-20 patients on every daily operating list. This was not helped, when the other house officer announced that, as a conscientious objector, he could not be involved in terminations of pregnancy (TOP). It was never a comfortable subject for me either, still a church going catholic at this stage. To compensate, the other guy did read the daily newspapers for me, while I did his list. To make it worse, the registrar at the time was also of the view that we needed to be doing TOPs only in exceptional circumstances. He had dared to question the boss's decisions on a couple of occasions, deciding against TOP in a few cases. The boss was furious, feeling that his authority was being undermined, and charged me the duty of watching the registrar to make sure this did not happen again. This put me in a virtually impossible position and resulted in my having to do even more procedures. During the many hours in theatre at Dulwich Hospital, I got to chat regularly with the anaesthetists, alias "the gas men". My regular one was a particularly quiet registrar, who had a reputation for not saying much and just getting on with the job. He ran into a bit of trouble, when, after 3 years in post, one of the consultants decided that it was time that he made an upward career move, something he had previously resisted. It was only at this stage that he was required to produce his medical documents. It transpired that he was not medically qualified but picked up his skills watching anaesthetists whilst working as a hospital porter. He subsequently began to help them out with ever more complex tasks, until it was assumed that he was one of the team. Despite 3 years without a single complaint, he ended up with a custodial sentence, creating a major scandal at the time.

Medical Registrar (Kings) July 1975 to July 1977.

It was July 1975, and I had the stability of a 2- year medical registrar rotation at Kings and Dulwich Hospitals. I was now much more in my comfort zone, where my skills were maximised. I now had house officers working below me and felt that I was making the important decisions on the ward and in outpatients. The second 6 months was Geriatric Medicine at St Francis Hospital which enabled me to have a hospital flat in the nursing home, rather than the constant hot bedding of the last 2 years. I worked under a very senior lady assistant specialist, Dr Raybould, who taught me that for geriatric ladies, the weekly visit from the hairdresser was at least as important the consultant ward round.

I moved on to 3 months at St Giles hospital and more general medicine. This was an old hospital destined for demolition shortly. I shared the staff accommodation with a rather strange psychiatry registrar, not that I ever met a normal one. Over the last few weeks of the summer, he had been abseiling down the wall of the hospital. I then realised that I had not seen him several weeks. I subsequently learned that he had been building a Morgan car from a kit in the downstairs changing rooms and had completed the job without considering how he would get it out the door.

After 12 months of general medicine, I moved over to Kings and the Maudsley for a joint Neurology and Neurosurgery registrar post with Professors Marsden and Zilkha, two of the most brilliant men I had encountered. In those days, we depended on traditional examination skills and subtle signs rather than routinely requesting an MRI scan and working it out from there. The disappointing aspect was that treatments in Neurology were pretty limited, and some cynics commented that there were only two types of neurological condition, amitriptyline responsive and amitriptyline nonresponsive. Amitriptyline is an antidepressant that blocks multiple neurological pathways, causing multiple side effects, some of which turn out to be beneficial, if you can put up with the others. At this stage, as a centre of excellence, we were seeing some of the first cases of Creutzfeldt-Jacob disease, later popularised as "mad-cow" disease. I presented a couple of cases at the hospital grand round and felt that I was something of an expert. The importance of this will crop up later. The second 3 months involved work on the Neurosurgical Unit at the Maudsley Hospital under Mr McCabe and Mr Polkey. This was the toughest 3-month period of my life. Essentially, we were on duty all the time, unable to even sleep in the normal doctor's residence, due to the number of high-risk patients. Nights were spent in a room next to the intensive care unit. Tell that to young doctors today and they will not believe you.

Most nights there would be a catastrophic head injury or intra-cerebral bleed admitted, which would mean an 8-hour operation, leading straight into a full day's operation list the next morning. As there were no house officers in neurosurgery, I was once again the lowest in the food chain. As the medical registrar on the team, my major role was in diagnosis and investigation with surgical duties were usually restricted to holding the retractor and managing suction. Eight hours of this during the night took its toll a couple of times when I fell asleep during operations and had to be "retired".

It was really around this time that I was able to afford to run a car in London and my first car was a Reliant Robin, not the status symbol at the time that it is now. Not many people realise that you have a 50% greater chance of hitting hedgehogs in a Reliant Robin which caused me great ethical concern. Another unique feature is that you can lock yourself out by simply closing the door having left the keys in the ignition. Luckily, a trick one garage showed me was that the construction was so flimsy that you can bend the locked door to get your hand through and extract the ignition keys. I was driving the Robin when I met my future wife, Sally at an infamous Kings disco and offered her a lift home. "So, you've got some wheels," she said, clearly extremely impressed. Luckily, she never asked how many.

Having experienced a few hairy drives over the Thelwall Viaduct, on the M6, I decide to treat myself to the relative luxury of a Citroen Ami, only one step above the 2CV. We all make bad second-hand car decisions at times, but after 3 months, I decided to clean the front mats, and discovered an expansive view of the road below. I was only slightly up market from a Fred Flintstone special. Imagine my surprise when the new American Senior Registrar, over on 6 months secondment, offered to buy the Ami from me. My relief was tempered with concern that I still had to work with this chap for 3 months. I should not have worried. On the same day that the money and the documents changed hands, some desperate thief stole the car from outside the Maudsley Hospital and wrapped it around some bollards on Coldharbour Lane. Clearly, they had not worked out that the left foot needed to be firmly on the road when braking at speed. The SR was extremely apologetic that he might have contributed to my "pride and joy" coming to an abrupt end.

It was during this post that the other Registrar, a proper career neurosurgeon, wanted study leave for his FRCS examination. Shortly after, I made a similar request to help with my part one MRCP exam. Not surprisingly, his application was successful, and mine was not, although I was given a morning off to take the examination. Not surprisingly, with 14 days continuous on call, I was unsuccessful, achieving a "bare failure".

The final phase of the rotation was 6 months as Medical Registrar on Accident and Emergency at Kings. Essentially, I was the initial resource for medical rather than surgical emergencies that presented. This post made me realise that an A and E post should be compulsory in every doctor's training. The immediate attraction of this post was the flexibility of the work, meaning that after a night shift, the following day was completely off duty. After 3 months at the Maudsley, this was bliss and I was able to step up my cricket for 1977, which was one of the hottest summers on record. I played so many games that season, I made over 1000 runs in several hundred hours at the crease. I managed to have my front teeth removed by a rather sharp West Indian quickie, which led to multiple attendances at the dental hospital over the next 2 years. Having resumed playing again, I was keeping wicket when a top edge removed all the impressive dental work, necessitating a full bridge and another 50 hours of dental work. I became a regular dental exhibit in the dental school for teaching and examination purposes.

Back at work, a couple of weeks into the job, a 6-year old girl was brought into A and E, having been electrocuted whilst playing on the railway lines at Denmark Hill. This was extremely distressing for all the staff as there were severe deep burns on the limbs from the electric wires. After repeated efforts at resuscitation and multiple shocks to the heart, the team wanted to give up, but, knowing that electrical injuries should carry a greater chance of success, I pushed on. Eventually we got a pulse, intubated her and after several hours work, transferred her to Intensive Care. Unfortunately, we had no idea as to how long her brain was deprived of oxygen. As I was still a catholic church goer, I ended my shift and headed off to the catholic church in Camberwell. To my surprise, the priest began the service with news about the young girl, who belonged to a staunch catholic family. He extolled the virtue of the doctors who had worked miracles to save her and the congregation united in prayer. I was reluctant to do so, as I feared the worse for the girl. Unfortunately, I never found out what happened to her.

Six months on and after lots of hard work this time, I went for the part one MRCP again, which is a multiple-choice examination with a low pass rate. I had never been good at multiple choice as I tended to over-think the questions but this time, I felt much better prepared. Of course, I achieved a clear fail this time, meaning I had only one attempt left. If I did not pass parts 1 and 2, then I had no chance of a worthwhile SR job. I decided to try the Irish MRCP part 1, which consisted of a traditional exam, with essays and case histories, rather than choosing a selection of answers. I was able to take this only 2 months later. Sally accompanied me to Dublin for the exam. We were on a very tight budget and stayed at the single star Harcourt Hotel in Harcourt Square. The unwelcoming foyer belayed the hovel that greeted us on the 3rd floor. I decided to have a bath (not en-suite) after the ferry crossing only for half the masonry to fall on my head. I retired to the bedroom. As I relaxed my hand went down the side of the bed and I felt an article of clothing. This turned out to be a mummified pair of string Y fronts. Luckily, we were only booked for one night.

As it was a Sunday, I did not want to miss worship, so Sally accompanied me to the local catholic church. The priest that day would not have been out of place in an episode of "Father

Ted". He began by destroying the concept of church unity by announcing that Non-Catholics were not welcome in his church. I detected that Sally was on the verge of walking out, but I urged her to stay. The collection arrived, and I emptied a considerable number of coins (punts) from my pocket onto the collection plate – quite generous I thought. The priest then announced, "It has come to my notice that some parishioners are putting coins onto the collection plate, may I remind you that they will answer for that in hell fire". Rather steep, I thought. At this point we were both on our way. On that day, I think Sally was turned off the Catholic church and I think that my attitude also changed.

At the Royal College in Kildare St the next day, the exam papers arrived and to my pleasant surprise, the long diagnostic case was clearly Creutzfeldt-Jacob disease, my pet topic. This was manna from heaven. It made me realise how much luck plays apart in our lives. I later learned that the pass rate for this exam was only 17% and I was one of the lucky ones. Three months later, I returned to Dublin, not surprisingly choosing a different hotel. I passed the part 2, first time as I realised that exams involving patient communication skills were to my advantage.

As I was waiting for the right job to arise, I spent the next 6 months doing locums around London and there was plenty of work as I could handle, Medical, A and E, and Gynae posts. It was interesting working in over 30 different hospitals around London. Some nights my bleep would go off and my first thought was "Who am I?", rapidly followed by "Where am I?" unsure of which specialist I was and where I was working that night. I remember a SHO Gynae post at the Prince of Wales Hospital, Tottenham, where I fell in with a couple of Australian anaesthetists over a very quiet weekend on-call and lost more money at poker that I had earned in locum fees.

I found myself on duty in A and E at St Stephen's Hospital, Chelsea, when an IRA bomber, Patrick Hackett, had planted 9 bombs in central London. One exploded prematurely causing him to lose a leg and part of an arm. It was very demanding having to do your best to save the life of a terrorist you had attempted mass murder, even one with the same name. I was hounded by the press all night, with repeated questions as to possible associations I might have with the IRA. Patrick was eventually sentenced to 30 years.

One night I was on-call Medical Registrar at St Mary's Hospital in London and for the second time that day, I was with the crash team for a resuscitation that was not going well. As I was giving chest compressions, I was looking straight in the eye of a patient across the ward and I could see that he was just about to arrest. I gave a decision to stop the immediate case and switch to the newly arresting patient. I doubt that he would have survived had we not been a few metres away at the very moment that he arrested. This was a case of third time lucky that day.

In April 1978, I was offered a 2-week post as medical house office at Bromley Hospital. I was taking jobs at lower grades as the money was still good. On my first ward round with the consultant, I already seemed to know more about the patients than the incumbent registrar. At the end of the round, the boss took me to one side as said, "You seems to be a smart chap, how would you like to be registrar?" He promptly dispensed with the services of the existing locum registrar, who had been appointed by hospital management. Three days later, he told me that he had be watching me closely and felt that I could be left in charge, as he felt that he could now take a long overdue holiday. Effectively I had been promoted from house officer to consultant in 3 days. There was little that I could do but to accept gracefully. Four days into my promotion, I was presented with a very complex patient who was going downhill, and I could not work out a diagnosis. I decided to approach the other medical consultant for his advice. To my surprise his response was “You work for that b*****d. He and I haven’t spoken for years, you’re on your own”, and walked out. Luckily, I was able to ring a consultant at the sister hospital who came over to help me out.

I was now applying for multiple further registrar jobs, focusing on top London Hospitals, along with Oxford and Cambridge. I was always getting to a final interview but my decision to take a job in gynaecology was being singled out as a sign of indecision. It was clear that some of the jobs were already a “done deal” for the local applicant. I could not even get a job at Cambridge which had come up early, because the previous doctor committed suicide. I decided to lower my sights and applied for jobs at 2 Manchester hospitals and interviews arrived for the morning and afternoon the next Friday. I decided to combine the interviews with a trip home to see my father in Bolton. I must have been more relaxed for these jobs as I was offered both, but curiously both sets of consultants felt that I should really be setting my sights higher, say London or Oxford. They suggested that I might be taking a backward step if I accepted the Manchester jobs. I followed their advice and declined both posts. Both hospitals declined to pay my travelling expenses.

I noted that the BMJ was advertising a registrar post in Renal Medicine in St Louis, Missouri working for a Professor

Hubert Lubowitz, with interviews to be held in London. Why not go for it, I thought, now or never? The interview went well, and I was offered the job. There was even some confidence that Sally would be able to get a job in Physiotherapy. I had passed my ECFMG, which, as far as I was aware, was the only examination required for the US, but, unknown to me, two new exams, FLEX and TRAB had just been introduced but there had been no formal sittings for them. I was therefore in the ultimate catch-22 situation. Professor Lubowitz rang me at home a couple of times and threatened to "kick-ass" at his end. Inevitably the job fell through. I made one more interview at Cambridge, only to overhear 2 female applicants discussing that they already knew that they had the jobs, and for one, it would fill in 4 months before maternity leave. That was the final straw. I felt that I was travelling all over the country just to make up the numbers. It was the summer of 1978 and I think I finally realised that a career change was required. I turned to the BMJ general practice section and spotted a GP partnership in Cheshire close to where my family had lived. I was also aware that in 6 months, 3 years mandatory training In General Practice was about to become compulsory. It really was now or never.

I sent off my CV to the practice in Holmes Chapel, failing to realise that there were more than 200 applicants. Most of whom had perfectly planned careers compared with my recent knee-jerk decision. After about 10 days, I had heard nothing, so I rang the practice, asking if I could come up and look around. I failed to realise at that point that I was being completely naïve. I clearly took them by surprise, and I arranged to go up the following week. In retrospect, I realised that my CV must have been rescued from the discard bin. Once again, I was about to discover that most important things in life are completely due to chance.

CHAPTER 4.
The Viagra Years and Beyond

It was the summer of 96, and the first patients from the sildenafil studies had returned for assessment. It was clear that at least half of them (50% had to be on placebo) were showing profound effect. It was becoming impossible to get them to return the unused tablets. This was a problem that I had never encountered before. I arrived home and stormed into the house, "Where is the number of that stockbroker?". Suddenly I realised that this might be considered "insider dealing", although things were less clear at that stage. There had been no problem whatsoever recruiting men for these trials, as only painful injections, were available previously. I was always aware of a vast difference between men and women in relation to drug trials. In the case of women, their bodies are *temples* and they need thorough information as to the absolute safety of anything being put into their bodies. In the case of men, merely telling them that, to date, only 5 rats had ever taken this medication would be sufficient, if at least one of the rats had survived. The trials involved being provided with unlimited medication to be taken prior to sexual attempts and then completing a "Sexual Encounter Profile" (SEP), with explicit questions about what happened to penis before and during penetration. There was also an "International Index of Erectile Function" (IIEF) Questionnaire to be completed at each visit. Later on, there was much criticism, as these questionnaires, developed in middle America, only addressed issues in heterosexual couples.

The Nineties were a golden age for clinical research, and it was a privilege to be involved right from the beginning in the development of a Nobel prize winning drug that not only changed clinical practice forever but is now a household name. We were also doing the studies on Invicorp, an injectable drug for ED, and I was still a full time GP partner in Lichfield. Work was great fun then. There were frequent clinical trial meetings, usually at pleasant venues in the UK, plus regular international meetings in Urology and Sexual Medicine. I often wonder why medicine has lost its attraction for so many doctors in recent years

Based on the development of sildenafil (Viagra) and similar drugs to follow, a new speciality had developed. Initially Professor Alan Riley had set up the British Erectile Disorder Society, aptly named BEDS. I was treasurer and charged with organising the inaugural meeting. I chose the Victoria Hotel, Stratford on Avon and handled all the negotiations with the hotel. Having recently attended a meeting on "Revascularisation of the Penis" in Madrid, where the huge banner outside the hotel had caused public consternation, I was concerned that nothing similar happened to the delicate residents of Shakespeare's Birthplace. I dealt with a lovely girl, Sharon, and rang a couple of days before the meeting in May 1997, just to check that there were no issues related to our "special" group. "We have had all sorts here" was her comforting reply. I was greatly reassured as we had about 80 delegates attending. Imagine my surprise when I parked outside the hotel in Stratford to see a huge sign outside saying:

"The Victoria Hotel, Stratford welcomes the British *Reptile* Society,". Perhaps her major concern was that delegates might be keeping snakes and Iguanas suitably moist and cool in the bathrooms.

BEDS only lasted about 18 months before being renamed the British Society for Sexual Medicine (BSSM) in line with the European Society for Sexual Medicine (ESSM) and International Society for Sexual Medicine (ISSM). Dr Bollinger was now a rising star in the Sexual Medicine world, displaying all the finest qualities of British Diplomacy to keep the rival Italian, Greek and Turkish factions in order. Whilst I was a hard working "serious" researcher, Dr B's flamboyant, eccentric, larger than life- style meant that he was destined for greatness.

By September 1997, the genie was out of the bottle and patients were aware that a "miracle" tablet was available. The clinic was becoming busy. This was excellent news for clinical trial recruitment for the trials as this was the only way to gain access to the new treatments. Although 50% received placebo, after 3-6 months all patients received active treatment for up to 12 months. Trials were also just beginning for tadalafil (Cialis) and vardenafil (Levitra) as members of the same class of drug, PDE5 inhibitors. As a "key opinion leader", I was also able to obtain medication directly from the manufacturer prior to the UK licence of Viagra in 1998, which gave the Good Hope clinic a significant edge. Things were going to change in September 2018, when the Department of Health brought in some draconian regulations to restrict NHS prescribing to contain expenditure on the miracle blue pill.

A "miracle" drug will also be associated with unrealistic expectations. Despite all the best advice, older men were still seeking to "surprise" their partners after several years of inactivity. They would take a tablet just before Match of the Day and expect a rustling in the trousers even during the dullest of 0-0 draws. If we could persuade them that both parties needed to get their kit off first and that they needed to rediscover the concept of foreplay, then they might have a chance.

By May 1998, the clinic had developed a bit of a waiting list as none of the patients on tablets could be discharged back to their GPs. To save time I was asking the nurses to get the patients to complete an IIEF score to assess severity of ED, An Ageing Male Symptom Score (AMS) and International Prostate Symptom Score (IPSS). I am a big fan of questionnaires as they get the patients to do a lot of the work and if I forgot to ask a question then I know that the answer will be there in one of the questionnaires when I come to write the letter. I used to look at these before referring to the GP letter to see how well they predicted the patient problem. Sometimes the process let me down badly. Horace Stapes was 73 when he saw me on 23rd May 1998. His questionnaires looked surprisingly normal, so I went back to basics,

"Now, Horace, what has brought you along today?"

"I'm having trouble with a buzzing in the left ear" he said. "Is it worse when you get an erection" I asked. "

"No but sometimes I am a bit deaf and I feel blocked up. I can't sleep". "Any trouble with libido or ejaculation?" I was now having to ask direct questions to make progress. "No, that's fine, but sometimes the buzzing turns to a ringing noise". Out of desperation, I decided to read the GP letter:

Dr. Benjamin Hardwick. MB.BS. MRCGP

The Bell End Surgery, 23, Bell End Lane, West Midlands, B65 9LP

Tel: 01562 623489 Fax 01562 632492

Dear Doctor,
Re Mr Horace Stapes, 14/12/38.
14 Crotch Crescent, Bell End, Worcestershire B65. 9LS.

Please assess Mr Horace Stapes who is being troubled with a severe bout of tin nuts.

Dr Benjamin Hardwick
GP Registrar

Not only had the GP's practice spell check badly let them down but somebody in the hospital appointment department had a strange idea of my clinic workload.

Many men thought that Viagra would make them instantly attractive to women. Some believed that every erection must end with sex and many thought that Viagra would roll back the years. Many women thought that it would turn their husbands into sex-maniacs. In reality, there were probably marriages only held together by the man's ED, but that was no excuse not to treat him. Some women in the US tried to sue Pfizer for their husband's infidelity, after they had been treated with Viagra.

Archibald Johnson, 63, presented in late 1998, following a series of heart attacks and a couple of failed cardiac stents. It took him nearly 5 minutes to walk the 20 metres from the waiting room and he was breathless for a full minute after sitting down. His wife, Cynthia, was 15 years younger and he found her very attractive but feared that he would lose her if he was unable to satisfy her. The great cardiologist Graham Jackson showed us that sex is a physical activity equivalent to walking a mile in 20 minutes and climbing 2 flights of stairs. Clearly Archibald's heart was not capable to the effort involved for sex. We discussed the issues, but he seems unable to comprehend that sex is dangerous for him. If he is walking and gets chest pain or shortness of breath then he can stop, but, at the height of erotic frenzy after a large meal and a bottle of Claret, he is likely to push on beyond his limit. Men often comment "What a nice way to go!" without realising the impact on the partner of such an event. Men in this situation often say that "Without sex, life is not worth living". Although the proper answer is to tell such men to forget sex, this advice will not be taken. In such cases, I believe that it is possible to negotiate with the couple, some form of limited sexual activity, where most of the work is done by the partner. It is crucial that the partner fully understands the risk and that this is documented in the notes. The paradox is that these drugs that we use for ED are actually very good drugs for the heart.

Sex after a heart attack is rarely discussed by cardiac rehabilitation nurses. Comprehensive advice is given about a date when hoovering can be safely resumed. I can assure nurses that none of these men in coronary care are thinking about when they can next get behind the controls of their Dyson Big Ball. In fact, in common with most men, I have spent most of my life trying to have as much sex as I can, whilst doing as little hoovering as possible. Every week in my clinic, I see a man referred after a recent heart attack. In nearly every case the ED commenced 3-5 years earlier and many chances were missed. Despite all the evidence, this situation has not changed significantly over the last 20 years.

Around this time, I returned home, and Sally broke the news that once again my son, Dan, was in tears following yet another detention. The project at school had been to construct a poster on "How to look after your heart". Whereas the other children had cut out pictures of men exercising, plates of healthy food, or bottles of vitamins, Dan had attached a box of Viagra. They had failed to appreciate that my son was years ahead of his time. His punishment was another 2 weeks detention. Life was tough for the family of a Sex Tsar.

Nicholas Dingle,70, was a former Barrister with a high sex drive. He had developed Parkinson's disease and was drinking more heavily since giving up work. His glamourous wife, Annette, at 52, usually attended with him. Penile Injections had been largely unsuccessful, but he now wanted to try the tablets. By trial and error, he worked out that 2 tablets and 1 injection did the trick. I constantly looked at Nicholas with his shaking hands and drooling from the mouth and could not really imagine the two of them together. Annette told me that, every night, Nicholas would book a taxi and head to the red-light area of Birmingham returning home after 3am, usually drunk and often shouting and unsteady. Her major issue was that her previously high-flying husband was now a complete embarrassment. I was aware that a common side effect of drugs for Parkinson's disease was hypersexuality and this was clearly the problem here. He was totally fixated by sex, but neither his GP nor neurologist were interested in any discussion about changing his medication. It was obvious to me that Annette was having a relationship with somebody else, but I had to explain that Nicholas was my patient and that my duty of care was to him and this was the life that he had chosen. I remember an 85- year old lady on multiple drugs for Parkinson's disease in a nursing home. She was frequently found on top of elderly gentlemen, having wandered into their rooms at night. I still remember visiting the home and catching her on top of this poor old chap, pulling at his todger whilst he was screaming and pressing the panic button.

The range of referrals to the clinic was rapidly changing. This was usually driven by the development of effective treatments. GPs were pragmatic and did not see the point of referring patients when they know that there is nothing that can be offered. We knew for some time that a lot of young men with ED did not respond to tablets because their testosterone was low. Nobody wanted to go on to injections in the penis, and we were finding that restoring the testosterone levels to normal not only stiffened the erections, but also improved their libido, energy levels and much more. We now had very effective testosterone treatments in the form of gels and long acting injections. Things were getting very exciting. GPs were realising that sending these men to Endocrinologists was largely a waste of time as patients were seen by junior doctors who just repeated blood tests until the doctor moved on to his next job and then the new Doc could take over and request further tests. Many of these men with low testosterone were belated referred with infertility. In the NHS, a couple who are not conceiving will be referred to an Infertility clinic, usually in a Gynaecology clinic, run by doctors who do may not have treated a man for several years. The role of the man is as sperm donor. His medical and psychological problems are rarely considered.

Sean (35) and Sarah (34) Goodfellow had been seeing Mr Bender, Private Gynaecologist in Harley St for infertility for 2 years. I had treated his ED well with daily Tadalafil giving him frequent morning erections. They were having sex twice daily. Previously their GP had been rationing Sean to 1 tablet per week on the basis of NHS guidance from 1998, based on a "No sex please, We're British" Survey from the 70s and 80s. Sarah brough a letter from Mr Bender that seemed to have identified the problem:

Mr Hugh Bender. MB.BS. MD. FRCOG

The Infertility Clinic. 147c Harley St, W1G6AQ 0121 623 7543

Re Mrs Sarah Goodfellow
3rd April 2009
79, Minge Lane, Upton-on Severn, Worcestershire. WR8 0NN.
03/07/75

Dear Dr Hackett,

I believe that Sarah's infertility is due to allergy to her husband, Sean's semen. She therefore needs comprehensive prick testing, which I have personally administered today. I will see her again in 2 weeks.

Yours sincerely

Hugh Bender.

Certainly, Mr Bender's personal prick test had done the trick and it was smiles all round, although I suspect that the daily Tadalafil was also crucial to success.

Despite the CCG embargo on accepting female referrals, my experience in research into female sexual dysfunction led to a limited number of referrals, often when I had Identified that the major sexual issue was with the woman. The immediate problem in treating woman is that the predominant problem is lack of *sexual desire*. This is common around the menopause but causes much more distress when it arises in younger women. The problem is often related to hormonal contraception. The high dose of oestrogen in oral contraceptives increases the production by the liver of "sex hormone binding globulin" (SHBG). The function of SHBG is to lock onto the oestrogen, rendering it inactive, and transport it around the body. The problem is that the SHBG has a stronger affinity for testosterone than oestrogen. Women have roughly 10% of the male level of testosterone, so the rendering of this SHBG bound testosterone as "inactive" produces significant symptoms, especially lack of sexual desire or libido. This can be treated with low dose testosterone patches and gel, but these are not licensed in women. Treating woman with low dose testosterone is very rewarding and I had been treating many women since 1999.

Rose was 59 and had been treated with bilateral mastectomies for breast cancer and hysterectomy and removal of ovaries for ovarian cancer. I had been treating her husband, David, with diabetes and low desire by prescribing testosterone gel and daily tadalafil with limited success, mainly because of the problems Rose was experiencing. The addition of a tiny amount of testosterone gel for Rose, had immediate effect and transformed their relationship. Their only problem then was that Rose was now more interested in sex but found difficulty in getting aroused and reaching orgasm. The addition of daily tadalafil to her regime made a huge difference. After 6 months, the dynamics of their relationship had changed, and Rose was now initiating sex and David was having difficulty keeping up.

I saw a very similar effect with Janet, 68, and Peter, 66. They both had type 2 diabetes and I was having moderate success with Peter but he was aware that Janet seemed to be getting little pleasure from sex and was extremely dry, a common problem for women with diabetes. The addition of a tiny amount of testosterone gel was effective, but it was only the addition of daily tadalafil that changed the picture. Peter commented that, by 3 months, Janet was a different woman. She had stopped her anti-depressant and become much more mentally alert, contributing much more conversation. She just seemed a much happier person. I have followed them up for 10 years and they still have an active sex life. In fact, Peter now struggles to keep up with her.

I was becoming very positive about treating more woman and approached the hospital management. An immediate problem had cropped up. Because both testosterone and tadalafil were “unlicensed” for women, the pharmacy and the GPs were refusing to continue prescriptions. I had been issuing private prescriptions, as I was aware of this issue, but it was pointed out that hospital policy did not allow the issuing of private prescriptions, so this had to stop. I have managed to transfer a few patients into the private sector to maintain the treatment.

> On reviewing my medical insurance, the following year, I discovered that my premium had been *doubled* as I prescribed *off label* medication!

More prescribing issues were emerging. The NHS was still restricting men to one tablet per week of the job with the lowest acquisition cost, pharmacist jargon for "cheapest". This was based on a UK lifestyle study from the 70s which revealed that married couples over 50 had sex once per week. They included the 50% who would have ED, which meant that those who could have sex did it twice per week. They applied this rule to all and made no allowance for younger, single, gay, or bisexual people. In 1998 they also introduced a restriction that only men with diabetes, Parkinson's disease, and a few other rare conditions, could get medication on the NHS. The rest had to pay inflated private charges irrespective of age or financial means. They also introduced a category of "single gene neurological disease" which was a mystery to all of us. The only disease of this type I knew was red/green colour blindness, so curiously I had introduced sight testing in the ED clinic. The most bizarre rule was that men suffering "severe distress" could be treated on the NHS but this totally new disorder can only be diagnosed by a consultant in a hospital and all drugs must be prescribed (indefinitely) by the hospital. When we operated in line with these guidelines, the Primary Care Trusts would impose fines on the hospital for failing to discharge patients within a reasonable period. Any sane person would see these rules as complete "bonkers", but we have been stuck with these for 22 years.

I mention this as on 5th April 2009, my first four referrals of the day of the day included a line from the GP, “I think that his problem is causing him severe distress”. My comprehensive test for this was to say, “Mr Donger, do you think your problem causes you severe distress?” Almost always, they had been primed to answer, “My God, yes doctor, every minute of the day”. The diagnosis was now clear, and this man would now be visiting the hospital pharmacy (at huge additional cost) indefinitely. Occasionally some patients had not been primed properly and answered, “I’m not happy, but severely distressed… probably not”. “In that case, Mr Pike, here is a private prescription that will cost around £60 per month”. Invariably the response was “You know doctor, on second thought, I am severely distressed, and the wife, she was so distressed, she was in tears when I left the house today”. At this point I would tear up the private one and issue an NHS script.

If the reader thinks all this is rather strange, the last of these patients was actually referred by myself from my own practice. Yes, I saw patients in my own practice and wrote a referral letter to myself. Six weeks later I would greet them at the hospital and confirm that I totally agreed with their GP (me) that they were suffering from severe distress and provide a NHS prescription so that they could make the regular 30-mile round trip to pick up their tablets from the hospital, indefinitely. I would then dictate a letter to myself “Dear Doctor Hackett, Thank you for your excellent referral letter, I totally agree with your diagnosis…” Occasionally I commented that I was so impressed with the standard of the referral that I suspected that I must have had additional training!” My secretary expressed concern when she read some of these letters, strongly suggesting that I might be losing the plot.

Restoring a couple's sex life can be the most rewarding thing a doctor can do. As a GP, I remembered many diagnostic successes but no matter how well you controlled blood pressure, cholesterol, or diabetes, this was rarely appreciated. In contrast, restoring a man's erections makes him a friend for life. Not only that but his wife would hug you if she saw you in the street. Never have I had a wife shake my hand and say, "Lowering my husband's cholesterol has changed our lives".

Unfortunately, some cases are not straight forward, as in the case of Aaron Schmuck, 28 and unemployed on long term benefits. Taking a full sexual history is vital in all patients. Aaron had never had a sexual partner but was complaining of ED, based on considerable masturbatory experience. Without being cruel, it was difficult to imagine that he was likely to have much success as there was little that I could see that would make him attractive to women. Five visits in, the daily tadalafil (under severe distress regulations) was giving him morning erections and he was successfully masturbating several times per week with the use of some heavy pornography. I decided to have an open conversation with him as to what more he expected from me. It was clear that he had hoped that his morning erections would be attracting women from near and far, but tactfully, I tried to explain that this was not going to happen unless he was proactive. Clearly, as an NHS consultant, I cannot arrange dating or escort services or even providing a number that I might have seen in a local telephone box (if you can find one). I hoped that he might have got the message, but he left stating that he would still like to see me again. Reluctantly I relented. Three months later, Aaron was back and still seeing success with regular masturbation. My advice had been partially successful as he had been visiting a local prostitute on 3 occasions and felt that there was some form of connection. He was seeking my advice as to whether I thought he should ask her out on a date. Of course, his idea was likely to be a complete disaster, but I did not want to destroy all his hopes at one foul swoop, so I answered, "Well it certainly worked for Richard Gere". Strangely, I did not see Aaron again. I would like to think that he carried his "Julia Roberts" off into the sunset.

As the clinic and GP work had been demanding, I was looking forward to teaching at a GP course in the West Country and an overnight stay with the Bollingers the night before. Dr B was always the most generous host, fine chef, and sommelier. We arrive at their country estate after the long drive and were greeted at the gate by Hector, their exuberant but friendly schnauzer. Mrs B greeted us, and we adjourned to the lounge for drink as Dr B was delayed at work. As the conversation was flowing, Hector climbed onto my head from over the back of the sofa. I was used to boisterous dogs at home, so I saw this as a sign of affection. By now Hector's teeth were just by my left ear and the familiar whiff of canine halitosis was evident. I noted that Mrs B was stroking Hector's testicles fondly. "Geoff, would you just mind checking Hector's left testicle" asked Mrs B. I spluttered on my gin and tonic, catching site of Hector's glistening fangs in close proximity to my left cheek. I contemplated how he might react to a strange hand exerting pressure on his left epididymis. I politely declined, reminding her that whilst vets can treat humans, strictly speaking, physicians should not treat dogs. Conversation continued until we noted that Hector was repeatedly scratching at his ears. I made the big mistaking of asking if he was OK. Mrs B informed me that the Vet had diagnosed eczema but after 3 visits and 3 different creams it was no better and had cost a fortune. She showed me the tubes of cream and it was pretty mild stuff. Sally then interrupted "One of our Labradors had the same problem and Geoff prescribed a strong cream for me on prescription and it worked a treat. This was a big mistake, as 5 minutes later I had issued a private prescription for Mrs B. When Dr B arrived home, we enjoyed a massive fillet of beef on the BBQ, several fine bottles of Claret and retired to bed rather late. As with most meetings after a night with Dr B, I just about coherent by 11am, the following day, a pity as my talk had been at 9.30. A week later I decided to ring and thank them for outstanding hospitality, and politely enquired how Hector was getting on. "Well," answered Mrs B, " I took the prescription to the chemist as you suggested and the pharmacist came out and said *the usual instructions are that, if you are using this on the nose, put a small knob on a cotton wool bud and gently apply in each nostril. For the ear put a small knob on the little finger and gently insert into the canal"*. "Actually, I'm putting in on my schnauzer", answered Mrs B. The Pharmacist replied, *"In that case I would recommend loose fitting underwear and no sexual activity for at least 48 hours".*

"Hector seems to have a lump on his left testicle, would you mind just checking it while you're here?"

In recent years, the clinics were full of health-conscious IT "consultants" who arrived with spread sheets of symptoms and blood results on their i-Pads. They approached problems in their sex life in the same way as they approach software issues, failing to realise that, where women are involved, no app had ever been devised to solve such problems. Adam Rutter, 38, was a fitness fanatic and ran his own website design company. He had suffered anxiety problems and multiple relationships had failed. He refused to believe that somebody running 100 miles a week could possibly develop ED. At his last visit, I had commenced him on tadalafil 5mg daily and, within a week he had noticed firm morning erections and multiple spontaneous ones during the day, especially when working with attractive girls. His first question was "Is it dangerous to go running when I have such a strong erection?" "Only if you run the 4x 100m relay". I replied. "No, more of a middle-distance man myself", he answered. Yet another piece of fine satire had missed the mark.

"I knew I shouldn't have taken a second Viagra this morning."

The first patient in my clinic on 25th June 2012 was Roger Shakeshaft, who was 34 and complaining of a sudden loss of libido. I asked about his wife and family, and he proudly announced that he and wife Tracey had 6 children aged 3,4,5,6,7 and 8. One might be tempted to think that a loss of libido might be long overdue. I was intrigued as to how he managed to afford 6 children in 6 years and inquired as to his occupation. "I'm a precision grinder" he replied.

In July 2012, a hospital doctor popped into my clinic to ask for a box of Viagra as it was his mate Steve's 40th birthday soon and he was planning a cunning stunt. He planned to leave a box of Viagra, with 2 tablets missing, in his bedside cabinet, in anticipation that his wife, Jane, would find it. I declined to co-operate and tried to persuade him that this was a bad idea. He ignored my advice and got hold of the tablets elsewhere. Things did not work out well. Jane found the tablets and confronted Steve, who denied ever using Viagra, even when Jane challenged him with her discovery. What the pranksters did not realise was that Steve and Jane had not had sex for a long time and Jane was highly suspicious that Steve was having affairs, no matter how many times he pleaded his innocence. Jane proceeded to become obsessional and constantly checked his phone and email accounts. Steve asked the prankster to tell Jane about the stunt, but this was the final straw. Jane thought that Steve had sunk so low as to persuade a friend to lie to get him out of trouble. Steve came home to find his clothes shredded and his suitcase by the door. A salutary warning for anybody prone to such cunning stunts. Luckily, having been kicked out of the house, Steve was able to move in with girlfriend.

In 2013, I was approached by the University of Bedfordshire with the offer of a Professorial post in the Department of Diabetes in Older People. There was actually a very small salary which was a pleasant surprise. The appointment was based on my research and publications around testosterone and diabetes. I soon realised that the real reason for this offer was my abilities to potentially generate funds from outside sources. It was no accident that I had recently secured the promise of a substantial grant. From my point of view, it was far wiser for the University to administer the grant, even if they took 20% for themselves. Little did I suspect that the accounting processes of the university were unusual. They were spending my budget on salaries for other projects, in the hope of generating future income. This effectively left nothing in the pot when vital payments were need for my research. The Head of Department concerned moved his unit to another university shortly afterwards, and my position was terminated.

In 2014, a case demonstrated the difficulty of dealing with myths and misconceptions. Alan Tickle, 72, and wife Tess,73, attended with ED, that had not responded to his GPs prescription for sildenafil. The letter stated that their daughter was assistant manager of the hospital Patient Advice and Liaison Department (PALS). Alan seemed fit, apart from some long-standing back pain treated with co-codamol intermittently for 5 years. My routine questionnaires suggested that Alan had symptoms of an enlarged prostate and possible low testosterone. His GP had checked his testosterone that was slightly low, and I rechecked it and found it lower still. A rectal examination was normal. I ordered a PSA (prostate) test as I would for all men of his age with low testosterone or prostate symptoms. I suggested that the GP commence some testosterone gel and daily tadalafil 5mg daily. I told them that the tablets would only work if his testosterone was treated at the same time, explaining that the low testosterone was likely to be related to all the painkillers he had taken. The couple told me that an active sex life was a high priority for them both. I returned from holiday 3 weeks later and found that his PSA was slightly increased at 4.5 and this was confirmed on repeat testing. Alan had only just received the prescription from the GP and used it twice. I advised that he stopped the gel and referred him to a colleague, who did a prostate biopsy which confirmed cancer confined to the prostate. He was successfully treated by a radical prostatectomy. Despite all the trauma, Alan and Tess seemed delighted that I had picked this up early and that he was effectively "cured" of his cancer, although he now had severe ED after the operation.

I was shocked when a letter of complaint arrived from the daughter, suggesting that I had prescribed testosterone inappropriately and that the treatment (2 doses only) led to prostate cancer. The myth is that testosterone therapy causes prostate cancer, when all the evidence, as in this case, is that *low* testosterone is associated with increased risk of more aggressive cancers. Because of her important position in the trust this complaint was treated seriously. Not only were her parents not informed prior to the complaint being made, but the daughter was totally unaware of the couple's request to treat the ED as a very important issue. Many daughters do not even consider the remote possibilities that parents in their 70s might still be having sex. The daughter had totally missed the point that prostate cancer develops over many years and his raised PSA tests predated testosterone therapy. The reality was that, had this couple not had the ED investigated with a testosterone level, the PSA would not have been done and the prostate cancer may well have been diagnosed much later. Six months later, Alan went on testosterone therapy, which enhanced the effect of the tadalafil, and they resumed an active sex life. Alan and Tess advised their daughter to withdraw the complaint.

In July 2015, Peter Crossley, 58, a past local major, attended the clinic having previously been under the care of a urology colleague who had recently retired. Peter had severe ED and had failed with all medical treatments. Having been on the waiting list for a penile implant for 2 years, due to lack of funding from his CCG, he was expecting more bad news. The week before, I had been discussing the lack of local funding with a good friend, and senior consultant at a London Teaching hospital. He informed me that they had a special training budget and they were keen for more cases. I told Peter the good news. He was seen on the following Saturday in London and the operation took place a week later. He and his wife, Kate have been delighted with the results. We often use them as a teaching case at meetings.

In the last few years, more funding for trans patients requesting full gender reassignment has been made available as this has been a hot political issue. A penile implant is the only solution for full female to male transition.

Not all cases have worked out as well as Peter, the previous case. George Nobbs was 79 and married to Norah for over 50 years. All medical treatments had failed but they were desperate for a solution. As George had been treated with radiotherapy for prostate cancer and also had diabetes, my colleague in London was reluctant to use an inflatable implant. George was offered a malleable implant that works like a "bendy toy", that is bent upwards for sex and then downwards the remainder of the time. The procedure was performed as a day case under local anaesthetic and all seemed to be going well. George and Norah seemed very pleased. Unfortunately, one morning he forgot to tuck it away after some morning activity, as he was in a hurry to drop his grandchildren at school. The bulge was noted by some of the mothers at the school and a complaint went into the headmaster. Subsequently a letter was sent to Norah's daughter. George and Norah were absolutely distraught.

Body image problems are an increasing problem, especially concerning penile length. In the last 25 years, I have yet to hear a man, as he gets undressed by the couch on a cold day, state "I'm afraid it's rather large". Despite showing them a mould of a "normal" flaccid penis at 4.59-inch and 3.66-inch girth, these men are never convinced. The usual problem is that the length is completely normal but just concealed in fat. The solution is not what they want to hear. The usual reason for presentation is a new partner, who might have had a well- endowed former lover. One wrong expression or a comment such as "Is that it?" is enough to cause a complex for life. I often point out to the man that there must be a reason why the other chap is an ex-partner whilst he is the current partner. The other culprit, contributing to body image problems, is the well-hung donkey in a packed locker room who insists on going through his 10-minute arse-towelling ritual at every opportunity.

On 25th January 2017, Hugh Janus, a 58-year-old bank manager, wearing a 3 piece-suit, had presented with ED. He was accompanied by his wife Ruth. A final year medical student was sitting in on the consultation. Hugh disappeared behind the curtain and undressed. I became aware of some strange "clunking" noises as he removed his trousers. On pulling back the curtain, I was not only presented with a collection of full-body tattoos, nipple piercing, but a set of 5 Nobrium rings running the length of his penis and connected by a long silver chain. I glanced across at Ruth who was trying to distance herself from the embarrassing situation. The student and I managed to keep a straight face and we decided to administer an injection into his penis as tablets had previously failed. This involved removal of the 5 rings, all of which pierced the penis through separate holes. He had a good result and he left cock-a-hoop, although Ruth seemed less certain.

There cases made me realise that I needed to keep up to date with body image trends by watching all 3 series of "Naked Attraction". Luckily, Sally records this on series link for me, so I never miss an episode. I recommend this programme as essential viewing to anybody with body image concerns. Couples of all sexual orientations choose would-be partners on naked appearance alone. I now know how to appreciate a "nice tidy growler" when I see one. A more recent must-watch programme, "Naked Beach" invites vulnerable people with body image issues to live on a Greek Island with naked people of all shapes and sizes. The objective is that they will strip off in public on Naked Beach after 7 days.

On 6th March 2008, a young man of 29, Paul Gherkin, presented in my clinic. He complained to his GP about ED, loss of libido, tiredness, and poor sleep. The GP prescribed 4 sildenafil which were ineffective. Paul did not have a girl fiend. The GP diagnosed depression and had prescribed 2 different anti-depressants that were ineffective. Very quickly, we picked up that he had been treated for testicular cancer aged 16, his left testicle was removed, and he was treated with chemotherapy. We found his testosterone was very low at 4 nmol/l. The normal level should be at least 12 nmol/l. He responded very well to testosterone gel plus low dose clomiphene tablets to preserve fertility. It was a pity that there was a lack of continuity in care, as a low testosterone was a virtually inevitable consequence of his earlier cancer therapy. The treatment for depression was inappropriate and he effectively lost what should have been the best 10 years of his life. Unfortunately, symptoms of low testosterone are frequently misdiagnosed as depression and treated inappropriately with medications that have severe adverse effects on sexual function. The tragedy of cases like this, is that we can never give those men back the years that they have lost.

Over the years, I have seen many doctors and health care professionals, who have self-referred to me, as they felt too embarrassed to go through conventional channels. I wrote up 10 of these cases, entitled "a tale of 19 testes", in a medical journal. In case, you are wondering, one of the doctors had only one testicle. I now present a few of these cases, to demonstrate how sexual problems impact quality of life, even for doctors!

Mahmood was a 38-year-old registrar in diabetes, who attended my clinic as part of his training. After sitting in on cases, I noted that he was nodding off, not a common experience during a dynamic session with the Tsar! On questioning, he reported the symptoms of tiredness, poor concentration, reduction in physical strength, ED, loss of libido and relationship stress were being reported by many men subsequently diagnosed and treated for TDS. He arranged for a total testosterone (TT) level to be taken, which was 7.1nmol/l, and pre-diabetes. He had a strong family history of type-2 diabetes. After two years on long-acting testosterone undecanoate (TU), his symptoms had resolved, he has lost weight, reduced his waist circumference by 6cm and his work performance has improved, with promotion and a research award at an international meeting. He subsequently took up a consultant post in India, where is one of few specialists treating men with low testosterone.

Alan was a 60-year-old GP with well-controlled type 2 diabetes, who attended a former colleague's practice. He had never been asked about, or mentioned, ED in more than six years. He felt, that since retirement, he was ageing prematurely and did not have the energy or enthusiasm to enjoy his lifelong passion for dancing. He was married to Jane, a sex therapist who attended a British Society for Sexual Medicine meeting and learned of the strong associations of type 2 diabetes with TDS. Diagnosis was confirmed with levels of 8.4 and 9nmol/l and he commenced long-acting testosterone injections, which he initially funded privately, but after several months he persuaded his GP to issue prescriptions. On contacting him two years later, he confirmed that he was fit, dancing regularly, and even peeing much better. He described his testosterone replacement therapy (TRT) as 'life-changing".

George was a 59-year-old doctor from Africa visiting on holiday and attending a teaching day on men's health. He suffered from type 2 diabetes, hypertension and chronic kidney disease and was investigated for anaemia in Africa with upper and lower endoscopy plus bone marrow biopsy, with negative findings. We found that his testosterone was low, but no other doctor had performed a blood test. He had attended with his 43-year-old wife, Jasmine, and it was clear that they had stopped sex more than five years ago because of his ED. This had caused her much distress. After commencing testosterone therapy (he obtained supplies himself), he contacted me to say that his anaemia had corrected within three months, he had lost weight and reduced his insulin and that sex, aided by oral medication, was now possible.

Raman was a 46-year-old neurologist with mild ED but reduced enjoyment of life and his sex life in particular. He felt that his marriage was at risk and his wife was constantly accusing him of having affairs (they have three small children). He tried sildenafil and tadalafil, but both caused headache even at small doses, with no improvement. He self-referred to my clinic and we found that his testosterone levels were marginally low. A six-month trial of testosterone gel was suggested, based on his symptoms. He noted improved morning erections and spontaneous sexual activity returned with no need for ED medication. His follow-up email stated that he was certain that the testosterone replacement therapy had saved his marriage.

Rashid was a 58-year-old consultant psychiatrist with type-2 diabetes, who was putting on weight and becoming tired, lethargic, and depressed. He consulted a fellow psychiatrist, who prescribed several antidepressants with moderate effect, and eventually advised retirement on health grounds. Only at this stage did he mention low libido and ED to his GP, despite suffering for five years, as the GP was a 'good friend'. He was referred as an NHS patient and found to have a testosterone level of 5.8nmol/l. Response to testosterone therapy was dramatic with 8kg weight loss, 5cm from his waist. Sexual function was restored with the help of daily tadalafil. He now had no regular job but returned to locum work as he felt "sharper than for several years". His major regret was that, over his psychiatric career, he must have missed several patients complaining of similar symptoms but who had only been treated as suffering from depression.

Ajaz was a clinical research scientist, aged 46 with type 2 diabetes (well controlled), body mass index 23.2, and long-term epilepsy controlled with medication. He went to his GP with low libido, tiredness, profound fatigue, and ED unresponsive to sildenafil. He was a regular long-distance swimmer and was forced to give this up. His GP took two testosterone levels which were very low, at 5.4 and 7.2nmol/l. He was referred to an eminent professor of endocrinology in

Birmingham. The letter he received from the professor stated, 'we see many diabetics like this'; 'we suggest lifestyle modification through diet and exercise'. He was appalled, feeling that his sexual problems were ignored. He commented that the professor looked as though he was usually at the front of the queue for the buffet. Ajaz subsequently arranged a self-referral to the Tsar, having read one of my papers. After two years on long-acting testosterone injection, his sex life was far better than before (now three times per week), with improved orgasm and ejaculation. It required considerable pressure on his GP to agree to prescriptions for testosterone and tadalafil. He was back to swimming, feeling much fitter and is working to a higher standard. His diabetes was well controlled. He had intermittently suffered from acne on his back and chest, which has required treatment while on testosterone therapy, but he saw this as a small price to pay. During Covid-19 lockdown, when he was unable to swim, he recently ran his personal best for a half marathon.

David was a 64-year old retired GP with type-2 diabetes whose wife, a sex-therapist had seen me speak at a meeting. Not surprisingly one NHS tablet of sildenafil was not satisfying their requirements and the headaches were the final straw. He had recently been diagnosed with severe neuropathy with painful, tingling feet, keeping him awake at night. As suspected, his testosterone was very low and the combination of daily tadalafil 5mg and testosterone gel not only solved his erection problems, it cured his neuropathy and sorted out his prostate problems meaning that he could stop the prostate tablets from the urologist that prevented ejaculation. He remained very well for 6 years until he returned with loss of strength in his erections and cramps in his legs. The urologist had recently added finasteride for his prostate, and this had reduced his libido. He was now on an ACE inhibitor and a beta-blocker for blood pressure. I suggested that increasing the tadalafil to 10mg a day would mean that he could stop the finasteride. I also suggested a switch of beta-blocker to nebivolol, as this is the only one that improves erections as the others make them worse. Unfortunately, top cardiologists are too busy to bother about erections unless prompted. Within 2-3 weeks his erections were back, the prostate was behaving and the cramps in his legs were gone. A junior partner in the practice told him that he could not have the tadalafil 10mg daily, as, according to the practice pharmacist, this dose should only be taken within 36 hours of anticipated sexual activity. David replied that he *always* anticipated sex within the next 36 hours and that it was only the tablets that the practice prescribed that seemed to prevent him from getting it. The young partner buckled under the pressure and handed him the prescription. Unfortunately, a non-medical patient would not have achieved the desired result. I spoke to David last week. He is now 75 and remains very well, having survived Covid-19 without needing hospitalisation. He now checks with me before accepting any new medications.

Reflecting on these cases, I wondered about the huge benefit for the patients of these doctors, as a result of restoring their physician to full function in their work. Clearly, if diagnosing and treating doctors with low testosterone results in such clear benefits, we should appreciate that many of our patients have equally important roles in society.

On 5th April 2018, Peter Wang, 24, had been seen by my colleague Dr Cole, with some very strange results with very low testosterone levels and no clear cause. I was reduced to saying "The only possible explanation for these results would be extensive use of anabolic steroids over many years. I know that Dr Cole asked about this but is it possible that you might have forgotten something?" Only after a long pause did he admit to many years of injecting anabolic steroids. I concluded that the job is hard enough without the patients making it totally impossible by withholding crucial information. Peter was living in fear that we would be judgemental and refuse to treat him. He was petrified that the truth would get back to his GP and ultimately, his family.

By February 2019, I thought that I had heard every name that a man could possibly give to his penis, when Ernest and Alice Slack, both in their 70s, appeared, complaining of problems with "Big Ben". On examination I was puzzled as to how they arrived at this name as "Big Ben" had clearly seen better (and bigger) days. I summoned up the courage to ask how they had decided on the name for him. "Well", replied Alice, "He always has 2 hands on him, he's only cleaned properly ever 15 years, and he hasn't seen any ding-dong since 2017".

By March 2019, I had over 1200 men attending the pharmacy on daily tadalafil 5mg under severe distress regulations and was the leading prescriber in the country, a title I saw as a badge of honour. Dr Milledge's old practice in Coleshill was the highest prescribing General Practice in the country. In every clinic I would see men for 6 monthly follow-ups as required by pharmacy regulations. All these men had failed with the traditional method of taking Viagra 1 hour before sex and were now essentially "cured" by taking daily medication. Most were having sex 3-4 times per week with total spontaneity. Many attended with their partner and the consultation went something like:

" How are the tablets going?",

"Great",

"Any new medical problems?"

"No",

"Any other questions?"

"Can I have more tablets please?" I would hand him the prescription; his partner would hug me and off they would go to the pharmacy. There can be few more satisfying experiences for a doctor than 2 people totally satisfied with the results from 1 tablet per day. Unfortunately, the Clinical Commissioning Groups were not seeing things this way. I was effectively being told that I must stop treatment that was highly effective and switch patients back to regimes that had failed repeatedly. This was the first time in my life that repeating a cycle of failure had been suggested to me as "best practice". Many of these patients had been surgically treated for prostate cancer. Getting sexual function back in these men can be extremely challenging. All my efforts and protests that this approach was not ethical were ignored. The response from senior hospital managers was "This is hardly a matter of life and death". Another pharmacy advisor suggested that I might be getting too involved with my patients and needed to "Chill out". More about that in the final chapter "Serious Stuff".

The regulations in relation to Testosterone replacement therapy were even more chaotic. The hospital catchment area included 5 different clinical commissioning groups all with different prescribing guidelines. These ranged from full co-operation with GPs taking over prescribing, to no prescribing allowed at all. The rest included different variations in "shared care protocols" as to what prescribing was allowed. One CCG insisted that the hospital must administer all medication until the patient was on a stabilised dose. This essentially meant that I would have to be at each patient's house as they rose and showered in the morning, ready to enter the bathroom to apply 4 pumps of the gel to his inner thighs before returning to my normal job. When I tried to explain this to a community pharmacist, her response was that this was not her problem. To make it worse, it was the post code of the GP practice and not the patient that decided which set of regulations prevailed. If we applied the regulations from one CCG of taking on all the prescribing duties, we would then be hit with a fine for failing to discharge the patient according to a protocol agreed elsewhere. Barely a week would go by with a letter arriving from a CCG threating some sort of action against me for breaching one or other protocol. Invariably the patient was caught in the middle of this pantomime totally unable to get reliable access to therapy that they needed.

At this time, the trust had been shattered by the repercussions of the Ian Patterson case, as most of his work was carried out at Good Hope and Heartlands Hospitals. Ian Patterson was the "Rogue Breast Surgeon", jailed for 20 years for 17 counts of wounding with intent in May 2017. This had led to a culture of "mistrust" and I felt that the annual appraisal at the hospital had become more of an interrogation process rather than constructive career development. As I was prescribing a number of costly medications "off label" and for perceived "recreational purposes", I felt vulnerable and under such intense scrutiny. It had become virtually impossible to deliver a progressive service under these circumstances.

In 2017, my excellent clinical assistant had to retire due to a severe health problem and management decided that I could manage without the need for a replacement.

A final straw was a letter from one GP practice who picked up a comment that I made when a retired partner and good friend had returned to part time practice. As he had attended many of our educational meetings, I wrote in a letter that it was great to have a "Men's Health Champion" back. This triggered a complaint to hospital management from the practice senior partner that I was being "unprofessional" for inferring that the other doctors in the practice were not interested in men's heath!

Since my departure from the NHS, I have been unable to escape the workload, as barely a day goes by without a desperate patient getting hold of my home phone number to seek help. It is very difficult to tell them that it is now inappropriate for me to be advising them.

Covid-19 lockdown has been detrimental to sexual relationships. I would use the following 3 cases as examples:

Stanley, 75, had been widowed in 2018, but in February 2020 had met a new lady friend but was seeing no sign of erection. He suffered from an enlarged prostate, treated with surgery. He also had moderate chronic kidney failure. A recent scan of his aorta had demonstrated a small aneurysm, but no action was required. His GP suggested that tablets might help his erection was wanted a specialist appointment to check if it was safe. Due to Covid-19, all routine appointments had been cancelled, and with ED being an example of the "most routine", he waited from March to June to find that waiting times were now over 26 weeks. This effectively means that Stanley would have to wait 9 months for a simple assessment as to whether a tablet was safe. He would spend this time in solo isolation, and it is highly unlikely that the new relationship would survive this time. Stanley has a limited life expectancy and he was being deprived of the possibility of developing a relationship that would be potentially life changing for 2 lonely people.

Patrick was a 76 -year old man with diabetes, widowed for 5 years. After a lot of investigation, I had eventually sorted out his ED and loss of desire with a 3-monthly testosterone injection and daily tadalafil. He had met Rose in late 2019 and they moved in together in early 2020. Due to Covid-19, his GP practice stopped all non-urgent treatment which included testosterone injections. As a result, his low sexual desire, tiredness, and low mood returned and his tadalafil ceased to work for his erections. Unable to see his GP, as only "urgent" cases were being seen, and will cancellation of his annual hospital follow-up, he stopped the tadalafil altogether. His change in mood and frustration with sexual failure was too much for Rose, who moved back into her own flat. Both Patrick and Rose remain in isolation.

Stephen, 28, was a very handsome young man with an excellent physique, who developed ED and complete lack of sexual desire after he was treated for 6 months with Roaccutane, a drug used for severe acne. He was treated with multiple antidepressants for 2-3 years, until he found his way to me, having read a paper I had written on side effects of these drugs. He had attempted suicide twice. After developing a complex regime of hormone manipulation, he wrote me a Christmas card in 2019, telling me that "I had changed his life" and that, for the first time in 5 years he felt motivated to meet girls and that a new relationship showed promise. In early June 2020, he informed me that the effect of lockdown and enforces separation had caused the relationship to fail. He had been unable to get his medications from the practice and admitted to feeling some suicidal thoughts. A GP on telephone consultation had put him on an anti-depressant, meaning that we were repeating the cycle of previous failure. The obsession with "R" numbers and Covid death statistics to the exclusion of all other health related outcomes will have considerable long-term implications, even beyond the cancer delays that are already being highlighted. Of course, as administrators frequently told me, "Sex is hardly a matter of life and death". In the famous words of Bill Shankly, in relation to football, "It is far more important than that!"

In 2018, colleagues felt that my work merited a current Professorial post rather than being "emeritus", a convenient term for a "has been". I duly attended an interview with the Dean of Aston University Medical School, with the exciting prospect of teaching at the new medical school opening shortly. Perhaps it was time for medical students to be taught something about sex by the Tsar? The interview went well, and the Dean seemed to be well in tune with my research and offered me the post, with teaching duties commencing when the first students arrived in September. He put me in touch with some of his research team and we began working on a project involving mice treated with tadalafil to assess changes in body fat. Time went by and I heard nothing, until I learned that the Dean had been escorted from the building and suspended indefinitely because of "inappropriate behaviour".

Recently I heard from Aston University and my position has now been ratified and the Tsar will be able to pass his experience unto future doctors.

CHAPTER 5.
The Sex Tsar and the Media

I was first awarded the title "Sex Tsar" by Men's Health magazine in 2005, when I was approached for a telephone interview whilst waiting at Sydney airport. The subject was the "health benefits of sex", a title very close to my heart. I must have been on top form as I was able to reel off all the facts that formed the entire basis of their article. The reason for the interview was a report that, after 4 years in a relationship, a man's quota of "nooky" begins to slip. This was a fine example of a wasted research grant to confirm the "bleeding obvious". Men's Health were looking for incentives to "recharge lust levels". I was able to update them of important research from Wilkes University in the US showing that regular sex boosts your immune system by 30%, presumably related to beneficial endorphin release. My favourite all-time paper was the Caerphilly Cohort study which appeared in a Christmas BMJ in 1997, showing men in the Welsh town who had *more than 2 orgasms per week* halved their risk of death from heart attack. I still remember the day that this paper was leaked to the media and the late great Terry Wogan commented:

"My God, she's trying to kill me". How true he was.

This paper suggests that the female (and male) partners of Welsh men hold the key to longevity. You are probably wondering as to whether masturbation counts, and the good news is that the orgasm is key. It gets even better as previous research showed no increased risk of blindness. Even moderate sex twice per week will shed 20,900 kilojoules per year, the equivalent of running 80km per year. This might seem irrelevant to any serious athlete, but it comes with minimal stress to the knees and zero chance of being hit by an articulated lorry. In the case of women, is seems that the quality of sex is more important but for men it is the quantity that matters most.

Researchers at Rutgers University in the US found that regular sex acts as a painkiller increasing blood flow to all parts of the brain during orgasm. As a sufferer of frequent migraines, I suggested this to my wife, Sally, as part of a clinical trial. She became suspicious after a month and terminated the study early. Although the activity was providing relief within a minute, she was becoming suspicious of the increased frequency of attacks, as they were now occurring daily. She suggested that I might try a regime of self-intervention in the spare room.

One of the most powerful pieces of research of all time came from the Royal Edinburgh hospital who examined 3500 people aged 18-102 (!). They found that those having sex 3 or more times per week looked, on average 10 years younger. This must be the most incredible finding in the history of medical research. It means that the fortune that we are all spending on cosmetic products, fillers and Botox can be replaced by a couple of extra episodes of "nooky" per week. In this case "solo nooky" is less effective as both parties benefit from each bonking episode. My observation was that the 102-year-old was probably delighted to look 10 years younger but the 18-year-old less so as his chances of "nooky "3 times per week might be reduced by now looking like a child.

My first excursion into the media was a readily forgettable appearance on "Kilroy" in 1999. This was a very popular daytime show in front of a live TV audience. James Kilroy Silk was a smooth silver fox who also had a controversial political career. The subject was low testosterone in men. The show was filmed at Teddington Studios in London. After a standard class rail trip to Euston, 5 of us were squeezed into a taxi for the hour-long journey to Teddington. After a few minutes, the slightly dishevelled man next to me, having over-heard that I was a specialist, began telling me his life history. Five minutes into the journey I was fully aware that he had a very limited sexual repertoire and suffered from ED, low libido, and retarded ejaculation. "Do you think it might be related to all the drugs I take for my paranoid schizophrenia?" he asked. I suddenly realised that displaying any sign of indifference to this man might be a bad idea. Seldom have I been so relieved to reach a destination.

The experts were taken to a different room before the show and Kilroy primed all the specialists as to when he would turn to us and what question we would be asked. I was very comfortable that I had 30 minutes to relax until my question. Soon after the live show started, it became clear that this was a complete set-up. There were several "plants" in the audience. They were there to report great responses to treatment received in a Harley St practice run by one of the experts. Fifteen minutes into the show, as I was just nodding off, having been on-call the night before, Kilroy suddenly turned to me: "Dr Hackett, it sounds as though the NHS is letting these men down badly, what is your response?". I woke suddenly, my first reaction being to point out this this was not my pre-prepared question, but I garbled a response that was incoherent nonsense. Strangely Kilroy decided not to go back to me for the planned question. My wife, Sally had recorded the programme and still brings out the tape at dinner parties when she wants to subject me to yet another ritual humiliation.

Just when I thought my day could not get worse, things went rapidly downhill. The return journey to Euston at rush hour took nearly two hours and no prizes for guessing who was sitting next to me. Even worse, the stress of the day or missed medication meant that his anxiety levels had increased. He seemed impressed by my performance, which suggested to me that he was almost certainly becoming delusional. On reaching the station, I bid him goodbye as I could see that the train to Birmingham was leaving in 5 minutes. "What a coincidence" he said, "I'm going to Birmingham, we can travel together". As we reached the train, I was getting pretty desperate; "I'm in first class," I said, and proceeded to turn right. Ten minutes into the journey, having been relieved of £85 for the full price first class ticket (money well spent, I thought), I was setting down to a gin and tonic and feeling soporific. I had drifted off into a relaxed sleep. I thought I was dreaming when I heard the announcement "Person on line at Rugby". My first thought that it might be somebody who had found today's Kilroy too much for them, but then the reality set in. We were being taken off the train at Milton Keynes and put on a coach to Birmingham. Fifteen minutes later, those of us in first class had the benefit of being first onto the coaches and suitably spread ourselves around the seats. There was a certain inevitability as to who was going to sit beside me for the 90- minute journey to Birmingham. This was possibly the worst day of my life. Twelve months later, I received a phone-call from Thames television inviting me back on "Kilroy" for a follow-up show. Without a second thought my response was "I'm afraid I'm cleaning the parrot's cage on that day". Strangely I was not invited again.

After the Kilroy debacle, I decided it was time for some "Media Training" as it seemed that a couple of the pharma companies had seen my performance and decided to sponsor my attendance at a 2-day course. The "experts" seemed to be ex TV interviewers charging £5k a day to teach doctors how" not" to answer any direct questions – perfect training for a would-be Conservative politician but not the Sex Tsar. I decided that I could develop my own flamboyant style.

My next opportunity came on Valentine's day in 2000, which seems to be a prime time for sex phone-in programmes on radio. My one take home message from the Media Training Videos was that I had the perfect face for radio. The first of these phone-ins was an afternoon slot on Capital Radio when I was paired up with a high- profile TV agony aunt and barely got a word in for 2 hours. I felt somewhat patronised and my views were dismissed because "As a man, I could not possibly understand a woman's feelings". This was followed by "men with sexual problems much prefer to see a woman as they are non-judgemental". I began to wonder if my whole life had been wasted inside a man's body.

The evening session on Talk-Sport looked much more promising – surely this would be an audience of real men who talk footy and drink lager. The evening was taking a similar pattern with a traditional Sex Therapist, with twinset and pearls, preaching avoidance of porn and more concentration of sensate focus. I concluded this must have been going above the heads of most of the macho male listeners. She made a couple of outrageous comments like "I'll only treat men with nice legs" and "I' wouldn't recommend Viagra for an older man unless he has a much younger wife". We seemed to have more women phoning in. Martha from Cockfosters was complaining that for

20 year that her old man had tweaked her nipples as if he was "tuning the TV". Much female laughter followed. Of course, as a man, I could not possibly give advice on seductive caressing of the nipples. I decided to fight back by recounting the story of a 50-year-old farmer, I had seen the week before, who complained that his wife continually yanked his todger as though she was milking a heifer. I still believe that as the possessor of a dick, I have more personal experience of the way it should be handled. As I left the studio, the technicians all thanked me for their memorable moment of the evening.

I would like to say at this stage that I love sex therapists, especially Trudy Hannington from Doncaster, the sex capital of GB, known in the tabloids as "Bonkaster". My other favourite is Angela Gregory from Nottingham, "a mistress of masturbation". There are others who are easily offended. I remember, after one meeting, getting raspberry reviews for using a comment that I had seen a 60-year old woman with a vagina "As dry as the Gobi Desert". I had taken the comment directly from the woman on one of the vaginal lubricants stands but somehow the statement became inappropriate coming from a man. Colleagues still remind me how I died on the podium that day midst gasps from offended therapists.

I remember a very senior Urologist, Clive Gingell starting a presentation to the annual sex-therapist (COSRT) meeting with his favourite cartoon slide of a huge penis on a drawbridge being carried by several soldiers. Whilst this was usually greeted by riotous laughter from medical students, this time there was stony silence – he realised that all was not going as expected. At the end, the lady chairperson thanked him with "We all greatly enjoyed your presentation, Mr Gingell, apart from the first slide which we found absolutely disgusting!".

On the afternoon of September 11th 2001, I was working from home, catching up on some football on the TV, when a female journalist from the US rang me for an interview on a vital issue that must have caused mental torment to all of us at some stage "The female prostate, does it exist?". Frankly, I had given up the search for the female prostate long ago, but I humoured her. The conversation drifted onto "G spot orgasm" when I suddenly noted on the TV vivid pictures of planes flying into the twin towers in New York. I tried to explain the magnitude of what was happening, but she reacted as though this was the lamest excuse for terminating a discussion that she had heard. Eventually I made my excuses, trying to digest what I was actually seeing on the screen. They say that we all remember what we were doing at the precise moment of historical events, but I guarantee that nobody else was locked in an intellectual discussion on G spot versus clitoral orgasm at the exact time of 9/11.

By 2003, the story was beginning to get around that ED was strongly linked with heart disease and that men should be encouraged to see their doctor at an early stage, and I was phoned by the Victoria Derbyshire radio show for a comment. During the interview she made an important observation, "I suppose that many men consult their doctor about a trivial matter and then reach the door and turn around with a *by the way* comment". Remembering my determination to adopt a flamboyant style, I quickly replied "Yes, this is very common. We call this the *hand on knob* consultation". There was absolute silence and the producer cut in saying, "Time for a traffic bulletin". In the break he told me that they were all glad that there was a lot of traffic chaos that day.

I now seemed to be the "go-to" man for most tabloid journalist and barely a week went by without a random phone-call from a freelance journalist at the Sun or the Daily Mail contacting me about some banal publication in an obscure journal. Invariably this was pre-publication and I had no idea what it was all about. Rather than hanging up, I always tried to give them a strapline for publication. In Summer 2005, I was in the middle of a busy surgery, when a call was put through from the Daily Mail and for some reason the new receptionist thought this must be put through instantly. The journalist was wanting some quotes on a new study on the increasing popularity of anal sex. I looked across my desk at a concerned mother hoping to have a discussion on the pros and cons of adenoidectomy for daughter Charlotte. I thought that the timing could have been better. Rather than be rude, I quickly replied "A colleague of mine, Dr Bollinger, has spent the last 5 years researching this subject. He is a world expert". I could sense the enthusiasm in her voice that, at last she had found a specialist passionate about anal sex. I think that Dr Bollinger was at a fundraising session for the village church organ when she rang him that evening. Although a fountain of most knowledge, I believe that Dr B also had only fleeting thoughts about anal sex. I think to this day he has never forgiven me for this one.

A call to send shudders down the spine came from a lady at Maverick Television, a company that was beginning to push back the boundaries of taboo subjects surrounding sex. The lady was assistant to the producer of a programme airing that week on channel 4 on the topic of "The role of furniture in sex through the ages". Once again it was in the middle of a busy surgery. An escape strategy immediately came to mind as I replied, "This is not my area of expertise, but I can recommend an excellent sex therapist who likes nothing more than to get her hands on a nice piece of Chippendale". I gave her the phone number for Angela Gregory. The lady had missed the subtlety of my response and rang Angela immediately repeating my comments about her love of a nice piece of Chippendale. Luckily, Angela seemed to take it in better spirits than Dr B. I think her performance on that show led to an appearance on a special X- rated episode of Antiques Roadshow.

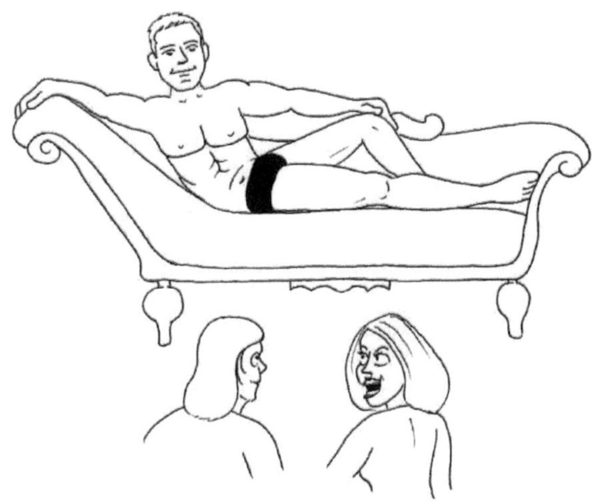

"There's nothing quite like getting your hands on a nice piece of Chippendale."

My major media debacle came on Sunday morning of 14th February 2007. I remember this well as it has been by son's 21st birthday and several of his friends had slept over after a successful attempt to totally empty my cocktail cabinet the night before. Sally and I had gone to bed at about 3am when the phone woke me from deep slumber at 7am. It was the producer of BBC news asking if I would appear live on the 9am news as a story had broken that Boots were going to make Viagra available in their stores. They could have a taxi at my home within 30 minutes. For some reason I will never understand, I accepted, only to realise that I had the mother of all hangovers once I assumed the vertical position. I slept throughout the taxi ride and the obligatory make-up session. For some reason I needed more than usual that morning. At home, my son had woken all his friends, and they huddled around the TV while Sally made bacon sandwiches. The BBC 9am news started and, as I was in a later slot, I was struggling to stay awake. Suddenly on came the lights and we were live. "My god, look at the state of him, is he asleep?", Sally shrieked at the TV. The questions were quite straight forward, such as "How does Viagra work?", "Is it safe?", questions that I could readily answer in my sleep. Suddenly, the newscaster asked, "And can you get it over the counter?" I paused for a couple of seconds thinking that rarely does one get a moment like this on the BBC live. At home Sally shouted "Please, please no!", as she saw a twinkle in my eye. I had decided to go for it "You know, I think I probably could". Strangely, not only was that the last question of the day but my last BBC appearance for several years. The good news was that I achieved instant "Legend" status with all my son's mates.

As President of the International Society for Sexual Medicine, Dr Bollinger popped up on our screens on "Dawn Goes Lesbian" on BBC 3 on September 6th, 2008. This was a 4 - part series featuring journalist Dawn Porter. The series commenced with "Dawn gets Naked", then "Dawn goes Lesbian", then "Dawn gets a Baby" and finally "Dawn gets her

Man". Dr B was the specialist who helped Dawn set strict rules, enabling her move in with lesbian housemates, work in a busy Soho Lesbian bar and culminating with the big question "was she up for a full-on lesbian snog!" Dr B was clearly addressing some of the most important ethical issues of the day. In an interview in 2013, Dawn listed this programme as the biggest regret of her career. She stated that "she cringes when she sees it, the programme was based on a false premise and she did it at a time when she didn't know how to say no to people". After speaking to Dr B, he clearly felt the same, but it you think that this was as low as one could get for Dr B, read on.

In 2009, Dr Bollinger and I were the only UK doctors to be involved in trials of a drug, Flibanserin, to improve sexual desire in women. We were invited to the company Headquarters in Berkshire for a media day, along with several other "thought leaders" in the field. We were split into groups for "brainstorming" sessions. The only problem was that Dr B and I had been out for dinner at an Italian Restaurant the night before with a few libations before and after. Although I had learned the hard way on several occasions that I was lightweight in his company, once more, I was struggling for the first hour of the meeting. Comments were made that I was "unusually quiet". The task for my brainstorming group was to identify the "perfect mature woman" as the "image "for Flibanserin. I was in a group of 6 that included Dr Dawn Harper, well known as one of the presenters on "Embarrassing Bodies" on TV. The rest of the group were coming around to choosing Kate Winslett as the marketing face for this drug, when I decided to strike a blow for common sense. For many years I have been enchanted by Fiona Bruce, such that I watched the 9pm news each evening merely to see what she was wearing. I never missed Antiques Roadshow and more recently I delighted in her weekly appearances on Question Time and my personal favourite, Fake or Fortune. Only a week before I had been watching her incredible cameo performance on Top Gear. I now thought that I would choose her as my specialist subject on Mastermind. Having contributed little to earlier discussions, I decided to make a robust case for Fiona Bruce above Kate Winslet. Dawn Harper prompted me with "Come on Geoff, tell us all why we should choose Fiona Bruce". "Well", I replied, "She was born in Singapore, educated in Milan, has a double first in French and Italian at Oxford, a further degree from Paris, happily married for 15 years, 2 children Simon and Mia, drives a Citroen Xara Picasso, goes to the gym 4 days per week and recently won "Rear of the year ……". "Woah Geoff, let's stop you there", said Dawn, "This is beginning to sound creepy; I think you might be Fiona Bruce's stalker, in fact I have a mental picture of you lurking outside of her house and popping up out of her bush!". The group were silent, as Dawn suddenly realised what she had said. From that day on, I cannot watch Fiona Bruce on TV without having a mental picture of myself popping up out of her bush. Three sessions of psychotherapy and hypnosis have failed to help. In case you are remotely interested Kate Winslett got the nod, but the process was all academic as drug has never been licensed in the UK, despite moderate success in the US.

My media appearances pale into insignificance compared with Dr Bollinger's larger than life epic performances. In 2013, at around midnight, I was flicking through the channels on the remote control and had skipped past the X channels when around 582, I came across a familiar face on Fiver 2 plus one. It was Dr B on the couch with 2 gorgeous interviewers talking with the recently crowned word masturbation champion, Masanobu Sato from Japan. He had recently regained his world title in San Francisco, breaking his world record with an impressive 9 hours 58 minutes performance. This was performed, of course without ejaculation, and extended his previous world record by 25 minutes. He was asked whether he thought that the elusive 10-hour barrier might now be within his grasp. He explained that to break this record he swam twice per week and had gained 5kg of muscle to improve his stamina. The camera cut to Dr B for expert comment on Mr Sato's training and dietary schedules. He dealt with searching questions as to whether altitude training might help, and whether WADA anti-doping checks should be introduced. For the first time, I saw Dr B completely lost for words, almost as though his agent had given him no prior warning of the subject matter. He pulled it all together by the end with some key tips on technique to reduce the risk of friction burns. I rang him the next day to congratulate him on his performance, "Oh God", he replied "I thought I'd got away with that". Luckily, I have the programme recorded as I am sure that is no longer available.

For those who may be interested, the 10-hour barrier was broken in 2018, by a 40-year-old bisexual American aptly named Drake Hardy (yes, his real name), who had broken the barrier several times in training before eventually officially slashing the record in front of a live audience. He commented that his secret was muscle control through tantric principles. He had even broken the 10- hour barrier with a partner but commented that she had required a short break every 2 hours. For those who might have thought that winning the Rugby World Cup in 2019 was the South African sporting highlight of 2019, think again. In December, Zakhele Xulu claimed the 2019

World Masturbation championship in Toronto and with it the Jonny Sins Cup. His margin of victory was only 45 seconds and asked whether he was ever worried that he might not win, he commented “It was touch and go at one stage”. I was offered a front row seat as medical expert for the final but decided that the second row might be safer.

In 2015, I was twice approached to appear on Embarrassing Bodies on Channel 4 (as an expert not an exhibit, to avoid any confusion). Having seen the programme many times, not only did I see this as potentially attracting the wrong sort of publicity, but I felt that I could never face Dawn Harper on camera without think about Fiona Bruce’s bush. As I stated earlier, I was now even more convinced that I had the ideal face for radio.

In August 2015, I was approached to lead an advertising campaign for a new drug for Premature Ejaculation (PE) called dapoxetine and marketed as Priligy. It was clear that the NHS would be reluctant to fund drugs for this condition and therefore a public awareness campaign was required. The theme was “Firing too Quickly”. The Media relations came up with the idea of using top rugby players. I often wonder how much drug companies pay marketing agencies for these ideas. The TV advert for” Firing too Quickly” involved 2 matches in bed, supposedly involved in “nooky” and after seconds one of them strikes and the flame brings things to an abrupt close. The message is that 20% of men suffer from premature ejaculation and help is available by going to the “Firing too Quickly” website. The 3 rugby players, deliberately not named, but still current internationals in 2020, were very quick to point out that they did not suffer from PE. They were clearly there to get the message across that even the most virile men could suffer from PE. I suspect that they really turned up for the fee, which I hoped was better than mine. They certainly earned it for listening we me witter on about PE for 20 minutes. The following morning, it was up at 7am for a radio phone in with Dr Hilary Jones, a true gentleman and definitely my favourite TV doctor. We had a great morning dealing with men's sexual issues, an infinitely better experience that earlier sessions with sex therapists.

One of the advantages of looking a bit old and craggy by 2019, was that I was passed over for some projects in favour of younger, more photogenic experts. One such programme was "My Sexual Fantasy" for Channel 5, immediately put onto series link as compulsory viewing for the Tsar. One of my trendier colleagues from BSSM, Dr Anand Patel has now emerged as the media's sexual fantasy specialist. In this programme, several subjects describe their intimate sexual fantasies, for the expert, Dr P to interpret. In a recent episode, one young woman described fantasising about older rich men taking her forcefully and displaying their worldly sexual skills. Dr P was skilfully able to explain everything in terms of her sexual frustrations with past relationships. The second case was a "hunky" man from Barbados who lusted after elderly well-spoken ladies for slow seduction in the women's wash rooms. I was less convinced with his explanation that this was a healthy guilty pleasure. Other cases ranged from fantasies over casual lesbian encounters to a man with a long beard seeking mass "dogging" experiences on public heathland. The reassuring message from Dr P and the resident sex therapist was that such fantasies were healthy and should be embraced, with no feelings of shame. This was very reassuring for me after weeks of sleepless nights fantasising that I was trapped in Fiona Bruce's bush with no prospect of escape.

A friendly journalist from the Sun contacts me on a monthly basis for comments on several subjects ranging from Botox injections for premature ejaculation, vaginal rejuvenation, surgery to restore virginity and the sudden popularity of penile lengthening operations. I have been happy to provide illuminating opinions which usually accurately reflect the conversation. In September 2019, he contacted me about the increase in NHS Penile Implants from 550 per year to over 900 and asked for possible explanations. I explained that this was probably due to several factors. As GPs had been paid to screen for ED, especially in men with diabetes, more men were entering the system, meaning that there would be more who failed, whatever treatment we offered. They, therefore, needed the ultimate "last chance saloon" treatment. In addition, increasing cases undergoing gender transition meant that prosthesis was needed for the female to male patients and therefore increased funding was available for surgeons to conduct more operations. He seemed to take all this on board and thanked me. The following night my younger son arrived back from a stag weekend in Prague. His mates on the plane had all picked up their free copies of the Sun. The front-page headline that greeted them was "BIONIC BONERS ON THE RISE", followed by most of my comments, suitably misquoted.

I had now achieved "legend" status with yet another group of young men.

CHAPTER 6.
International Travels with the Sex Tsar

Life as a Sex Tsar comes with the burden to provide education around the world. This became evident in 1992 when, along with Dr Bollinger, we set out to educate general practitioners on the importance of sexual medicine. At the time, GPs were responsible for collecting their own CME points. They received a grant and it was their responsibility to choose a balanced education programme. It was clear that, attending a 5-day residential course in Rochdale could be more expensive than a winter trip to Spain or Portugal, where doctors would also be able to recharge their batteries and engage in open air physical activity such as Golf and Tennis. On these crucial concepts, Medi-links was born and, over the next 11 years, annual courses to Spain, Portugal and France provided balanced education to over 700 GPs. Regulatory changes in 2002 brought an end to these conferences. Many doctors have contacted us since confirming that they remembered the trips with great fondness, some as the best experiences of their lives, some as events that changed their lives. Essentially the education was over 6 days with 6 hours per day, usually in the afternoons. The sporting activities were usually in the morning to ensure an early start to the day, as might not have been the case on dark winter mornings in Rochdale. There were many highlights to recall from these meetings.

The project got off to a disastrous start with the collapse of our chosen courier, Air Europe, the day before our first meeting, but somehow, after 24 hours on the phone, Medi-links manager, Sally, turned it all around. We featured many key opinion leaders, who might not have been attracted by an invitation to Milton Keynes on a winter morning. I have switched to the example of Milton Keynes to avoid offending the inhabitants of Rochdale and other great northern towns. On the second conference at Quinta do Lago in Portugal, entitled "The Thin End of the Wedge", we had Professor David Southall, a high- profile paediatrician from Stoke-on-Trent, involved in child protection. He produced evidence for his theory that many "cot death syndromes" were in fact Munchausen by proxy, the condition where mothers inflict deliberate harm on their children to gain attention. He produced evidence from covert surveillance cameras. The audience was transfixed, as they clearly had not expected such cutting- edge topics. Professor Southall subsequently became one of the most controversial figures in UK medicine over the next decade. The funding from his department was withdrawn as this was not the message that the funders wanted to hear.

A major advantage of the format of this conference was that speakers gave multiple contributions and were present for the entire week, mixing with doctors and contributing to sessions run by other specialists. Lifelong contacts and friendships were made, and a few even met their future spouses at these meetings. Such events would seem unlikely through a Thursday evening meeting in Basingstoke.

The agreement was that Dr Bollinger oversaw the academic programme and that I would handle aspects of travel, accommodation, and finance. One of the early Portugal conferences, entitled "The Quest for the Albatross" at Penina, in Portugal had gone quite well and looked as though it might be a financial success. We always ended with a conference dinner for around 70, featuring a set menu and house wine. We had met with the hotel manager and head of catering to discuss the arrangements for the "gala dinner" on the last night. The discussions were going well. We had discussed the place settings, menus, and wine, when the manager suddenly asked, "Would you like to dance?", Rising from my chair, I instantly replied "I thought you were never going to ask".

On the night of the Gala Dinner, I noted that Dr B displayed the familiar depressed face, edginess and mild sweating that always greeted the arrival of corporate chicken. I was confident, on this occasion, that he was aware of the business nature of the conference. Unknown to me, he had called over the head waiter and changed the 10-euro house wine to a personal favourite of his that he thought was "extremely well priced" at 70 euro per bottle. He failed to realise that our group of 70 usually managed a bottle each, meaning that he had essentially converted a nice profit into a moderate loss. At least we did get some excellent feedback on the wine.

On the return flight to Birmingham, all was progressing well and the 40 doctors on the flight were suitably relaxed. In mid-flight, an elderly lady was making her way down the aisle, when she began to stagger and slumped to the floor. There was complete silence as 40 doctors looked at each other, wondering who was going to leap forward to assess the situation. Would it be the Cardiologist or the Accident and Emergency consultant? Eventually, the consultant Gynaecologist stepped up and proceeded to examine the woman on the floor. One of the other doctors leaned forward and said, "How is it going, John, got a good view of the cervix yet?" Sometimes colleagues can be very embarrassing.

In 1999, we were back at Penina, Portugal, for a second time and I had invited my colleague in Urology from Birmingham, Mr Mike Foster. The meeting was entitled, "Reaching for the Pinnacle", reflecting our desire to achieve the highest standards in clinal practice. At past conferences, we had troubles with projectors, so this time we brought our own to avoid technical problems. On leaving Birmingham on our Ryanair flight, I realised that I had not booked in the additional baggage. A colleague suggested that I strapped it onto my back and then put my coat on over the top. I spotted the check-in attendant looking closely at me and wondering whether a request to remove my coat might reveal a severe physical deformity and cause great embarrassment. The ploy worked perfectly. I remember some years later that Frank Skinner on Room 101, demonstrating a special Ryanair Jacket that expanded to include 30kg of additional baggage. This was in response to a celebrity suggestion that Ryanair belonged in Room 101, perhaps the easiest decision Frank ever made.

Dr B had suggested that Mike Foster do a practical session on prostate examination. Mike brought his set of "ample buttocks" that included a rectum where different textured prostates could be inserted, to test the digital examination clinical skills of the group. We agreed that this was a great idea. Unfortunately, after 48 hours, Mike Foster had to go back to the UK, leaving Dr B and myself to conduct the prostate symposium. We were seated at the front of the hall with the ample buttocks on the chair between us, facing the audience. We were slightly surprised that some of the audience members seemed to see this as a photo opportunity. I later discovered that the photo had appeared in Pulse Medical Magazine as a caption competition, with the winning prized presented for

"The Arsehole is the one on the Left". I would like to point out that I was sitting on the right. The session went very well, and many well-educated digits were inserted during the 2-hour session.

When it came to the return flight, it fell to me to return the ample buttocks home to Birmingham. Unfortunately, the transit box could not be found despite an intensive search on the last day. This meant I would have to carry them on the plane. This time, I think the Portuguese check-in staff were too shocked to dare question why a hunchback was walking in a strange way, wearing an overcoat in 27-degree heat, carrying a pair of large buttocks. I was given an aisle set to guarantee maximal embarrassment. If the person sitting in the middle seat of that Ryanair flight from Faro to Birmingham happens to read this, I unreservedly apologise. Nobody deserves to sit next to a hunchback with a set of huge buttocks in their hands for 3 hours. I certainly noticed that, as people came towards me on the way to the toilet, one glimpse of the ample buttocks caused them to turn and use the loo at the front of the plane.

Between 1997 and 1999, I had been having some success on the golf course, mainly the result of a carefully selected pairs partner. I also had some individual success by winning the "Doctor Golfer of the Year" on the first and last year that the event was held. I had qualified at a regional event and managed to prevail in the final at the Belfry, with a 3-wood, over the water into the 18th at the Brabazon to set up a birdie. It never ceases to amaze me that we forget 90% of the medicine that we knew, but we can still remember individual golf shots, and they get better year by year. I won a 4-figure cheque for a medical charity, my hospital's special care baby unit. The reason that the event was never held again was that a lady qualifier returned home with stories of the fabulous hospitality to her fellow GP husband, who had failed to qualify. This grumpy chap complained to the pharmaceutical regulator and the company were heavily fined - incredibly sad, not least for medical charities. The good news for Medi-links was that the company concerned then switched their sponsorship to our overseas meetings. They clearly enjoyed living on the edge.

After the next course in La Manga, Spain, with the theme, "Soaring with Eagles", we achieved sponsorship for the First European Conference on Sexual Medicine at Penina, Portugal with many of the leading European experts attending as speakers. Dr B had come up with the innovative idea that we would hold the "Pfizer prize in men's health", worth £500 with the winner being invited to present their work at an international symposium sponsored by Pfizer later that year. The plan was that the doctors would conduct some audit or research in their practice in the months prior to the meeting and deliver their presentation at La Manga. Dr B and I had seen the 3 entries beforehand and they all looked reasonable, but we were taken by surprise by a "late entry" from one of the doctors, who I had already spotted as a "loose cannon". It was the overwhelming view of the group that he should be allowed to present his work even after the official closing date for entries. As the first slide appeared, it was clear that he had a big problem! His hypothesis was that he did not merit the Pfizer prize in men's health but that it should go to Harold Shipman! He then presented a load of graphs of performance targets comparing men and women in Dr Shipman's practice with the national average, concluding that Dr S was the only physician in the UK to achieve better outcome for men versus women, especially in terms of mortality. I felt incredulous that an experienced GP could have contemplated anything in such bad taste. I glanced across at Dr B and the look on his face was far worse than I had seen after even the worst corporate chicken experience. Luckily, we had agreed on a secret ballot with the results being presented at the gala dinner the following evening. A preliminary look at the votes suggested that we were in for a difficult time suggesting to Pfizer management that their prestigious men's health award was destined for Harold Shipman. This would be a certain end to any future sponsorship and the end of any future Medi-links conferences. At this moment, I witnessed what a superb diplomat Dr B can be in a grave crisis. Surely even the Brexit negotiation would have been safe in his hands. Luckily, the delegates had voted for a first, second and third choice. Although our joker clearly had the leading number of first votes, possibly even canvassed at the bar the night before the meeting, Dr B was about to deliver the master stroke. By applying the voting principles of the Tory leadership election and removing the votes of the last place candidates each time, he managed to find the one formula by which the joker could be pipped. The equation that he applied meant as much to me as the Duckworth-Lewis principle, but the right result was achieved. We had dodged a huge bullet. Never would we make such a gross blunder again. Unfortunately, once free places had been provided by sponsors, it became difficult to get doctors to fund themselves in subsequent years.

The final blow to overseas conferences came with a "First Tuesday" documentary on ITV in 2001, which dealt with the "perception" that doctors were enjoying "jollies" at the UK tax -payers expense. The under-cover journalists had planned an "ambush" at a medical meeting at Hillside Golf Club near

Southport. This involved a Thursday afternoon golf competition on my half-day, with doctors funding golf themselves. After the golf, two cardiologists presented some important findings from a new trial in the 45 minutes before dinner.

In the afternoon, I was playing the 5th hole and had pulled my drive well left. Luckily, I found the ball sitting up but had a very tricky shot to bend it around a large bush in front, and back to the fairway. As I contemplated the high degree of technical difficulty in the shot, I heard a rustling noise and felt certain that the bush in front had "moved". I reset myself for the shot and the same thing happened again. I stood back and moved forward to check this ambulatory bush. I was well aware from past experience that nasty things could pop up out of a bush. Suddenly a chap with a microphone popped out and asked, "As an NHS Doctor, how do you feel about enjoying this championship golf course at tax-payers' expense with the NHS in crisis?" Yes, it was in crisis even then. I tried to explain that this was my half day and attempted to produce my receipt to show that I had funded myself. This clearly was not the story they wanted, so they moved away. Unperturbed, we carried on, until the 16th hole, when I faced an exceedingly difficult chip over a bunker to a tight pin position, when another ambulatory bush, rustled on my back swing as another journalist appeared. This time my playing partner provided a few choice suggestions as to how he might shove a tree iron up their bush. They rapidly withdrew. After a shower, we adjourned to the restaurant to hear the speakers. The session went very well, but as dinner service began, the rear doors burst open and cameramen surged into the room. They focused intently on the food on our plates and contents of our glasses. Some 15 minutes later, after patient negotiation, they left the room. Although my excellent recovery from behind a moving bush did not feature, the programme produced the usual one- sided argument. The knee jerk reaction from the NHS was that all future meetings with a "perception" of leisure activities were no longer acceptable.

The European Society for Sexual Medicine (ESSM) was formed in 1995, and the Tsar has attended every meeting until missing Ljubljana in 2019. In addition, the International Society for Sexual Medicine commenced in 1998, holding meetings every 2 years in more exotic locations. I have missed only 2 of these. There are African (ASSM), Asia Pacific (APPSM), South American and Latin (SLAMS) and North American (SMSNA) societies. The British Society (BSSM) meets twice a year and in addition there are Urology, Andrology, Endocrinology and Sexology meetings. Sexual medicine is still thriving with a packed meeting calendar.

In 2008, Dr Bollinger set up the ESSM Summer School at Oxford University preparing doctors for the Fellowship of the European College of Sexual Medicine, the only acknowledged specialist qualification in the subject. Delegates from less wealthy countries could apply for grants to help develop sexual medicine in their own countries. The doctors, and the faculty would stay at Oxford Colleges for 2 weeks to experience the unique atmosphere. A feature at the end of long sessions, was "pub of the day". I remember long summer evenings with world experts such as Irwin Goldstein from San Diego holding court in the student pubs of Oxford. Suddenly Irwin would come out with a term like "clitoral orgasm" and the busy pub would become silent, with a pregnant pause, waiting for the next gem of wisdom. No other medical specialism could have this effect. Eventually, due to a combination of political and financial pressures, the school was moved to Budapest. The courses and examinations are now heavily oversubscribed, all due to the vision and hard work of Dr B, a true legend.

Many of these meetings merge into each other after all these years but some live long in the memory. At ISSM in Perth Australia in 2000, I had arrived back from an overnight flight from San Francisco and straight onto a long Air Brunei flight to Brisbane accompanied by Dr Bollinger. To make things worse for him, this was an alcohol-free flight. Luckily, a re-fuelling stop at Darwin at 4 in the morning allowed Dr B some rapid libations. This led the bar tender to comment “Struth, you pommy bastards aren’t as bad as I thought”. On arrival in Brisbane, I had the worst jetlag ever. I switched on the TV to see, to my complete surprise that they were just tossing up for the first test between Australia and West Indies at the Gabba. I rang Dr B in his room and confirmed that he was clearly struggling as well. One hour later we were at the Vulture St end at the Gabba enjoying a few” stubbies” with the locals, who took Dr B to their hearts, knotted handy, thongs and all. That night I had arranged to meet my aunt and uncle plus 2 cousins at their home in the Brisbane suburbs. Dr B offered to take some priceless photos of this rare family reunion. Cousin Michael arrived with his 2-seater Jag and somehow, we squeezed Dr B’s mighty physique into the back seat. Only later in the evening did we realise that Dr B had forgotten his camera.

We moved on to Perth for an excellent conference. I can remember a debate where, as a speaker, I was driven onto stage on a vintage Harley Davidson – those were the days. The test matches had moved on to the WACA and we took in the second test with WI bowled out in a session with a hostile Glen

McGrath hat-trick. Dr B now seemed to enjoy his cricket. On the sporting theme, I decided to play golf with an eminent diabetic specialist, Bill Alexander as he had managed to get us an introduction at the select Royal Fremantle Golf Club. Having played a number of "Royal" golf clubs previously, I realised that they were sticklers on proper dress code, so I arrived in long tailored shorts with knee length Pringle socks. I was already doubting the wisdom of the decision on the putting green, as the temperature hovered around 42 degrees and I was sweating profusely. Suddenly, the young assistant professional came out and announced that a few members had clubbed together to buy me some short white ankle socks as they could not have me going out on the course "looking like a complete poofta!".

At dinner one night in Perth, Dr B once again had that unmistakably disgruntled look on his face, and this time it was not due to corporate chicken. A urologist from Kettering had appointed himself as wine-buff for the evening and was going through a series of predictably pretentious tasting manoeuvres. Eventually he had chosen a young South Australian Shiraz and Dr B was not impressed. He asked Dr B if he was getting aromas of blueberry and avocado. Dr B casually replied, "If I was seeking the perfect enamel remover for teeth, this would be right up there!" Five minutes later he was discussing wines from the vintage collection with the chief sommelier.

Dr Bollinger can be prone to extravagant impulse purchases and this time it was a Didgery-Do, which he assured me had excellent sound quality. I could just picture a rendition of "Sun Arise" emanating from his Devon estate on Summer evenings. He was worried about excess baggage on the return flight, so I told him a tip I had learned. We obtained an old golf bag from an Aussie doctor and the Didgery-Do fitted in snuggly, alongside the 2 boomerangs, that were also too good to miss. I told him that Aussie airlines never question a man with a golf-bag. At the check-in, an old lady in front was grilled intensely and charged excess baggage but Dr B cruised through. He needed prompting from when asked which courses he had played whilst in Australia. At the AUA at San Antonio in 2005, Dr B had similar problems with impulse buying, with the purchase of a 10-gallon hat, Cowboy Boots and Spurs, plus a large deep fat chicken fryer. I was not able to help him on that occasion.

Four years after Perth and ISSM was in Buenos Aires. Dr B suggested a few days at an Estancia, a country estate, a few hours' drive from the capital. After a 13-hour flight, we travelled into the centre of Buenos Aires to pick up a car, only to find that Dr B had forgotten his licence. I discovered that I would now be driving through rush hour traffic and then cross-country. Dr B offered to map read and give directions, but I later learn that he has right/left dyspraxia and red-green colour blindness. This effectively meant that when he said, "turn right", I had to translate this into a left turn and when it came to traffic lights, I was on my own. On leaving the city, we came across thousands of people dressed in light-blue and white shirts and I thought that there must be a Bocca Juniors home fixture, when, in fact, it was a polo match. I was astounded how popular the game is in Argentina. The drive up the River Plate was like a trip along the Thames on a lovely summer day, with Eights rowing on the river and multiple equestrian events taking place. It was clear that we were not on the Thames when we stopped for food and the total cost was around £5. After 3 hours, we arrived at El Candelaria, a beautiful country estate. We had a flat each for about £30 per day, including 4 meals per day and unlimited access to a fine wine cellar, regularly explored by Dr B. I then discovered an adjacent golf course, and the professional provided me with clubs and a trolley as well as playing 18 holes, only expecting a drink at the end. Dr B was an excellent caddy, especially for refreshment duties. I have vowed to return to that wonderful place one day. It was then back to Buenos Aires for a wonderful meeting.

I remember in 2008, at the height of Dr B's term as President of ISSM, he was just about to make his presidential address, following his third visit to the magnificent presidential buffet. His plate was piled high and he was simultaneously holding 2 wine glasses when he was victim of an embarrassing malfunction in the trouser department. Dr B has always had a physique well designed for braces. On this occasion they popped. and his trousers fell briskly to his ankles revealing a fetching pair of red and white spotted boxers. For an awkward moment, he must have faced the difficult choice of "let them go" or "release the food". For Dr B, there was never any doubt. He waddled back to his seat to a standing ovation, not a drop or a single crumb were spilt.

At the American Urology Association in Orlando in 2008, tadalafil (Cialis) was reaching its peak, with new licensed indications. I had several key meetings to arrange, and most were on the golf course, to ensure 4 hours protected time. We stayed in a resort that was based on Porto Fino in Italy. The sponsor gave 4 urologists VIP tickets for Universal Studies, meaning that we could push in at the front of the children in the queues. The highlight was the X-men ride where the four of us were in a rocket ship shooting alien invaders with ray guns. The mandatory photograph was collected at the end. It was 10 years later that my son found the photo with the scores of each of us shown beneath our pictures. He commented that the others had scored between 50,000 and 100,000, whereas I was minus 100,000 meaning that I had the gun the wrong way around. I had been shooting myself in the groin for 15 minutes.

At dinner one evening, which in Florida is around 6pm, service was terribly slow. Dr B spotted a famous cigar emporium across the road and enticed me to join him. I have absolutely no interest in cigars but had resigned myself to sitting with a cup of coffee while he indulged himself. Within minutes, he had the manager in attention, and lots of sniffing was going on. Thirty minutes later, we wandered over with several boxes of fine Cuban cigars. He seemed embarrassed. "Slight problem, Geoff, no credit card". Such was my faith in Dr B, that I blindly handed over my card and the deal was done. We went back for dinner and, somewhat later, back to the hotel. I thought nothing more, until 6 weeks later and safely back home. Sally wandered over to me, as I was working and politely asked, "Is there something that you ought to be telling me?" I felt a sense of terror, as I thought what she might have discovered and what confessions were required. I started out with revelations over an expensive evening at the Spearmint Rhino, followed by 2 sessions of Swedish massage from the new masseuse, Inga. Clearly these were not the reasons, and I was in big danger of disclosing some even darker secrets if I continued. "Your secret cigar habit, $1999 worth", she replied, showing the latest credit card statement. I gave a huge sigh of relief that no more confessions were required. I contacted Dr B to arrange re-imbursement. He assured me that they were worth every cent.

I was lucky to be invited to do several lecture tours with stark contrast, from the peaceful tranquillity of the Gulf of Oman to the chaos of Mexico City, Cairo, and Jakarta. I particularly remember my trip to Indonesia. Jakarta was a highly dangerous place. I had a company representative with me the entire time. There was also my own dedicated driver in a red BMW, who waited outside the hotel and moved forward whenever I came to the front door. He drove with one hand on the wheel and the other on a baseball bat, especially in traffic. I even had my own butler, who offered to unpack my case on arrival. Rapidly, I remembered that I had been on the road for a week and my underwear had seen better days. I decided to spare him of all duties, including drawing my bath. Perhaps I should have asked him whether I should dress to the right or left, as this was information that would later prove useful.

On my half day free in Jakarta, I asked of the possibility of a round of golf. This was arranged at the city's country club. I was accompanied by the representative, driver, and a female caddy. I was paired up with a local businessman, who was firing golf balls all over the place but, luckily his caddy always found them, perfectly teed up. I had been playing reasonably well but, on the 9th hole, out of the blue, I produced an enormous slice, sending the ball into some very wild terrain. The two lady caddies raced on ahead and miraculously my caddy had found my ball, with a perfect shot to the green, although strangely the ball had changed colour from white to yellow. I duly converted my good fortune into a par, and we approached the halfway house for a break. My opponent duly went through a door with his caddy and my caddy made a gesture to me as if she needed a sleep. Rather innocently, I asked "Not tired already, surely". My opponent and his caddy emerged after 15 minutes suitably refreshed, following some adjustments to clothing. I commented that he played much better on the back nine. He explained that, at halfway, his caddy had straightened his shaft and thoroughly cleaned all his grooves giving him better grip.

The weather was getting very sticky, and there were a few rumbles of thunder and a suspicion of lightening. The last few holes were flood-lit, and I had pulled my drive closed to a floodlight post. As I positioned myself for the shot, up against the post, there was a flash of lightning and I felt a tingle pass through my body. That was it for me. We headed straight for the clubhouse and a warm shower. I was intrigued by the sign, as we entered the showers... NO BODYGUARDS PAST THIS POINT.

From Jakarta, it was no to Sydney for the Asia-Pacific Sexual Medicine Conference, which was a great success. On the last day, a Saturday, I was enjoying a farewell lunch in the sunshine at Darling Harbour before moving on the airport for the long flight home. I had foolishly booked a full day of patients back in the UK from 8.30 on the Monday morning. As we were finishing lunch, I became aware of a man staring at me from the waterside. Eventually, he wandered into the restaurant and politely asked, “Is it Dr Hackett?”. I nodded. “I hope you will be back in Sutton Coldfield for our 8.30 appointment on Monday morning”. I replied, “Yes, but will you?”

The next tour of duty was Russia in 2006, to present recent data on daily tadalafil in ED or so I thought. On arrival at Moscow airport, I was given a handwritten sheet of paper, carefully torn off a larger sheet. I was told that it was always imperative that I kept this with me. I arrived at the Marriott hotel at 9.30 for a lecture and press conference. At the hotel check-in, my single case was taken to my room. I was charged for 2 nights at £350 per night as I had checked in before 11am, even though I was leaving around 2pm. Local law dictated that the room had to be paid by the individual, not a company. I never actually saw the room; it merely stored my case for a few hours. The talk was assisted by interpreters as was the press conference. The only questions I had from the press all related to surgical restoration of virginity, not my area of expertise but an extremely hot topic in Moscow, if not in Tamworth. From that day, I have never experienced a UK patient requesting virginity reversal.

At 2pm it was time to pick up my sheet of paper and get an Aeroflot flight to Ekaterinburg, the 4th city of Russia, a 1500km flight from Moscow. The major tourist attraction in the city are the steps where Tsar Nicholas II, his wife and 5 children were brutally murdered in July 1917. I was surprised to see an audience of over 100 for my talk. The Chairman, who had seen me speak before, introduced me by saying, "We very much look forward to hearing from Dr Hackett about strange British activities such as *A bit of how is your father and shaking hands with the old lady's best friend,* not forgetting *a bad case of chaffing Chalfonts".* I had concluded that explaining cockney rhyming slang to Russians is as pointless as educating Americans on cricket's LBW laws". The interpreter was doing well in keeping up until I slipped in an unscheduled comment, "Sending a man with a rigid erection back to a wife with a vagina as dry as the Gobi Desert is not a recipe for connubial bliss". There was a stony silence as I later learned that there was no possible Russian translation for this. Once more the food looked promising but was completely tasteless. I concluded that the Russians must have an elaborate gadget for taking all the taste from food. I decided that I have no particular wish to return to Russia and certainly no desire to fly Aeroflot again.

In 2009, I was invited to join a prestigious group of experts on the newly formed GOLD panel (Global Opinion Leaders of Distinction). This was sponsored by the manufacturers of Uprima, a drug for ED with questionable efficacy. The first meeting was at Claridge's in London with the welcome dinner at the Café Royal. After a fine breakfast, the meeting started with everyone going around the table with their thoughts. An eminent speaker from Paris, kicked off with the statement "What I am hearing from my patients, it that this treatment does not work. What is the point of a fast onset of action if it does not work?" I slipped a sheet of paper in front of him which simply said, "I was at least hoping to make it through to lunch".

I remember a similar meeting at Cliveden, a magnificent country estate North of London, famous for the Perfumo affair. I had been working late and arrived about 11pm. I was greeted at the desk with the news "Ah Dr Hackett, you are in our premier rooms, the Prince of Wales Suite. Here is your butler to take you there". He took my case and I followed. On the door, it said Mr and Mrs Hackett. I thought, "What a surprise, perhaps Sally will be in the bath, surrounded by rose petals,". I realised I was now entering the realms of fantasy. As I followed the butler in, we both turned our heads to the left, to see a couple lying on the bed with sheets in a state that suggested recent activity. As I stopped, the woman opened her eyes, half asleep. For some reason, the only thing I could think to do was to give a pathetic wave. She shut her eyes again and we made a hasty retreat in reverse. Eventually, I was shown to my standard suite and slept well. At breakfast next morning, all was clear when I saw the woman again. Her husband was wearing a shirt with my designer label, HACKETT, embossed across the front. I have only ever been able to afford a pair of boxer shorts with my own label. Mrs Hackett clearly recognised me but appeared confused, clearly wondering if she had been dreaming the night before. For some reason, I gave her the same pathetic wave. I hope that even to this day she believes she was dreaming. After all you do not expect unwelcome intruders at £1,000 per night at Cliveden.

There have been several hotel incidents on tour. On a busy trip to the far east, I had been staying in a different Hilton hotel every night for a week, often uncertain of my current country of occupancy. I had been out for dinner in Bangkok and returned to the hotel, at around midnight unable to find my room key. I put my hand in my pocket and confirmed to the desk clerk that I was in room 408, unfortunately that was my room card from the night before. Of course, everybody trusts a slightly confused Englishman abroad, so he handed a card for room 408. I opened the door and immediately turned right for a quick pee, letting rip at the same time, muttering something akin to "better out than in". I turned for the bed, slipping my card into the holder causing the lights to come on, revealing a terrified Thai couple in bed. Another hasty reverse exit was required. Much worse happened to a colleague, who, after a late night had requested room service for breakfast. Completely naked, he opened the door, checked all was clear, and reached for the tray. Unfortunately, it was slightly further away than he realised. His foot had been holding the door open and, as it stretched, the door closed behind him. He looked on the plate for something to hide his modesty and settled for a piece of multigrain toast. Further down the corridor, he managed to find a morning newspaper outside the room, glad that broadsheets were still popular in Thailand. The lift down to the lobby stopped at every one of the 18 floors. Several people looked to him to press the button for desired floors before it became clear that both hands were occupied. Of course, at reception, the queue was 10 people deep, as a large group of school children were just checking out, but the manager kindly promoted him to the VIP desk.

In 2010, I made my second lecture tour of South Korea with 3 venues and 2 nights. The meetings were at 5-star hotels for the local delegates, but being from the UK, I was only permitted 4-star accommodation. This meant an additional 2-hour trip from my isolated flat to each venue. The talks went well, even with translation and the Korean people were very friendly. Each night we had a grand 8 course Korean Banquet. I could not understand a word on the menu, but I was sure that dog's testicles were there somewhere. The first course looked suspect, but I had learned how to handle these situations from an old Mr Bean film. I created a distraction and disposed of it in a floral display in the centre of the table. "Delicious", I uttered as the empty plate was removed. The second course looked safe but the 3rd one looked very risky. Whilst everyone was looking at the entertainer, I deposited the contents into the computer bag of the doctor next to me. I was now feeling safe, and slightly peckish, when course 4 arrived. It looked appetising so I tucked in. The doctor in the next chair turned to me and said. "I see that you are enjoying the dog's testicles, the sauce is delicious". On the last night, I luckily found a British Pub in the hotel basement, the "Rose and Crown", serving chicken and chips in a basket.

"Mmm, these spicy Korean meat balls really are the dog's bollocks."

In 2011, I was invited as International Guest speaker at the Brazilian Urology Association in Brasilia, the rather soulless administrative capital of Brazil. I was the final speaker of the session. The previous speaker droned on and even started singing at one stage. Eventually, they ran out of time and I did not even make it to the podium. On the following morning at 6.30am, I was giving an inspiration talk on "The role of primary care physicians in sexual medicine". I had spent many hours doing background work and preparing slides. As I started, I became aware that the only person in the audience was a cleaning lady, searching for debris under seats. I would like to say that, due to my inspirational presentation, she gave up cleaning for a career in sexual medicine, but I doubt it. Two Japanese doctors arrived just as I was finishing. This particular conference was clearly not a career defining moment.

In contrast the Chicago ISSM of 2012 was an academic highlight, when I was awarded their most prestigious research award, the Zorgniotti-Newman prize, for my work on low testosterone in diabetes. Two weeks before the meeting, I had been contacted by an old patient of mine, who had found that the Invicorp penile injections that I had prescribed were the only treatment that had ever worked for him. He had recently moved to the US and had been unable to obtain the drugs. I could see no solution until he mentioned that he lived in Chicago. In a crazy moment, I offered to bring 24 doses of the drug as I was out for the conference. As I was queuing to enter the US at Chicago airport, I noted a sign about bringing drugs into the country. It pointed out that importing drugs for the purpose of sale was a Federal office liable to prison sentence. I reasoned that my only defence was that they were for "personal use" and declared them on the customs form. The Officer checked my bag and had many questions about how the drug worked. I was quite certain that he must have a problem himself. He then spotted that I was only in the US for 5 days and yet I had 24 doses for personal use. He commented "Hoping to have a good time are, are we sir?" For once, I could not find a suitable reply. He allowed me through.

During the meeting, I attended a session on testosterone therapy for men, where a highly eminent urologist from Belgium was suggesting that men starting on therapy should have a rectal examination before, 3 months, 6 months, and 12 months after starting medication. I asked a question from the floor as to whether this was unnecessarily intrusive, and perhaps wasteful of precious specialist consultations. His response was rather unscientific. "I always like to show the patient that I care for their prostate". I replied, "In my case a simple Christmas card would suffice".

At the Chicago meeting, I spotted a desk with special deals on educational DVDs dealing with sexual problems. I thought that these would be useful to load out to patients. As I had ordered 4, including "Sex positions of the Kama Sutra", the sales lady, announced at the top of her voice to a packed hall that, with 4 purchases, I had qualified for a "special edition of advanced oral sex" free of charge. My efforts at an incognito purchase had failed miserably. As she was calculating payment for my card, she remembered and again loudly pronounced, "I almost forgot your free copy of advanced oral sex" just in case some in the hall were not aware. I then learned that I could not take them with me. They would have to be shipped to my hospital by discrete courier service. It was 3 months later that the DVDs appeared on my desk at the hospital. The package had been opened by several departments in the hospital. Most of the hospital porters look at me in a different light now as if they know me to be an exponent of advanced oral sex.

I accompanied Dr B, to Chicago's premier outfitter for the larger man. As I sat on the couch, and Dr B ordered most of the store, I was flattered to be told by 3 different salesmen that there was nothing in the store that would fit me. This gave me great confidence as, just before the trip, I had been to a traditional UK tailor. Having been asked "Does sir dress to the right or left? which I have never really understood, he followed up with "What waist size is sir wishing?" I answered," 34 inches". He replied, "Isn't sir deluding himself?"

I always seemed to be popular in Scandinavia and for several years was a regular visitor to their annual Andrology meeting. In 2015, this was in Helsinki. I had not been to Finland before and was surprise to find that my hotel suite had 2 saunas. I only discovered the second one when I took the wrong door on exiting and realised that it had been on maximal heat. I was told that evening drinks would be taken in the sauna before dinner. Everything that I had read informed me that such events in Finland are usually naked. I attended suitable undressed, to find that I was the only one to be making a stand-out appearance. Perhaps this might have been the reason that I was not invited in subsequent years, although I thought I presented rather well.

In 2017, I was invited to the faculty of the African Society for Sexual Medicine in Durban. I understood that some speakers had withdrawn, so I had to give 6 presentations, which was challenging. The health concerns and sexual attitudes are vastly different in Africa. They still have major HIV problems and some of the cases of Female Genital Mutilation were harrowing. I was very privileged to hear a first presentation from Mr Andre van der Merwe from Stellenbosch, who had recently conducted the world's first penis transplant on a 21-year-old who lost his penis after a cock-up circumcision aged 18. Botched circumcisions performed for cultural and religious reasons are a major problem in South Africa. The transplant operation took 9 hours and the presentation included video of the vital stages of the operation and serial post-operative photos. Within 3 months, the patient was urinating normally and could achieve an erection, ejaculation, and orgasm. Sensation was expected to take 2 years to recover but miraculously the boy had fathered a child within 6 months. My question of the surgeon was a serious one, "Why was he wearing the same underpants in all the photos?" He had not noticed; but rechecked the 6 slides and indeed they were the same boxers". "We all have our lucky pants" was his considered reply. This presentation took me back to one in Bangkok 5 years earlier, where a surgeon presented 350 cases of penile amputation. This is apparently a common way of dealing with a rival who has been secretly "servicing" a man's wife. Paramedics needed to be informed that "Penis was usually in garbage bin". This is crucial as the penis needed to be placed in ice and re-implantation carried out within 4 hours if function is to be preserved.

Although opportunities for International travel are not what they were, there are still regular European events. Most recently in 2019, I was at an event in Budapest, enjoying dinner in a restaurant with 2 reps from our pharmaceutical sponsors and 4 prominent urologists specialising in penile reconstructive surgery. They soon had their mobile phones out comparing photos of their favourite penile curvatures. They openly discussed the case of a paediatric urologist whose phone rang in theatre and he asked a nurse to answer it as he was scrubbed. His last activity on the phone had involved a penile curvature in a young boy listed for an operation the next week. The nurse was shocked as the picture popped up, and later informed the police. The surgeon was suspended for possession of pornographic images and took 6 months to clear his name and resume work. I was conscious that I was contributing minimally to this fascinating discussion, but I was aware that all conversation in the restaurant had stopped, and everyone was listening to us. At this moment, one of the reps produced her phone and showed us a series of "Dick Pics" from her Tinder account. Apparently at least 2 of these appear each time she arrives in a new European destination. Who said that romance is dead nowadays?

A number of these trips were associated travel chaos. I was on a Gulf air flight from Dubai to Singapore when the announcement came for a doctor. In an instant, the stewardess was alongside, informing me that one of her colleagues was in severe abdominal pain. My first though was whether my fillet steak and merlot would be saved, but I quickly responded. The announcement came over the address system that there was a medical emergency with a doctor examining the patient. A detour to Delhi may be necessary. There were load groans in all sections of the plane, especially from the Arab royalty in first class. I quickly assessed the situation. I was prepared for a pneumothorax as I knew how to relieve the pressure using only a straw, rubber tubing and a pen knife. This could have been my moment. The young lady was rolling around in pain from the abdomen. The history suggested severe Irritable Bowel Syndrome, brought on by her "cheating" boyfriend finishing with her the night before. Luckily, they carried an antispasmodic on board. I gave the thumbs up for the pilot to continue. I provided the girl with my own special cognitive behavioural therapy, agreeing that all men are b*****ds. I emerged back into my cabin to rapturous applause with a couple of the royal family members coming from first class to thank me personally. I believe that camels were offered, but no wives. When I arrived back in the UK, there was a letter of thanks from the airline for my consummate professionalism, but no mention of any business class flights, or the residue of my unfinished steak and merlot.

Some travel problems were more mundane. Many of the European meetings mean budget flights crowded with embarrassing young Brits on Stag and Hen trips. I remember one with KLM in 2015, when I had a tight connection in Amsterdam to catch a flight to Florence that just arrived before I was to give my presentation. At the airport, I had noted a large stag group dressed as "superheroes". This must have seemed a good idea at the planning stage but after 5 pints of larger before the 8am departure from Birmingham, it was looking like a big mistake. At security, none of them could find their capes and super weapons. Of course, they were on my flight, and by departure time, some were still lost around the airport terminal. I checked my watch, as my connection was going to be tight. I found myself sitting next to Captain America, who was looking very queasy. He was refusing to put his substantial cape in the overhead locker and the stewardess was making her point. Unfortunately, he then used some choice language and that was it. The stewardess now insisted that Captain America repeat the following words, "I apologise unreservedly and promise to treat the staff with the respect they deserve". Unfortunately, Captain A was so drunk, he could not string two words together. The whole plane was hanging on every word and after several attempts, he managed something approaching the script. We had missed several departure slots and we arrived in Amsterdam 2 hours late. For anybody interested Captain America vomited twice during the flight, both thankfully into the paper bag. From my point of view, my trip to Florence was now pointless, and after 8 hours at Amsterdam airport I was on my way back to Birmingham. My case enjoyed 3 weeks in Florence. KLM have a record second to none in losing luggage, over 50% in my case. Their standard letter of response to complaints informs you that they only have the staff to respond to 20% of complaints and unfortunately this time you have been unsuccessful.

Over the last 5 years, opportunities for international travel have diminished, even for the Sex Tsar. Trips to international meetings need to be self-funded such that only eccentric millionaire doctors can afford to travel. I am sure that the Tsar has the genuine sympathy of all readers.

CHAPTER 7.
The Sex Tsar in General Practice – More Art than Science?

I arrived in Holmes Chapel, Cheshire in November 1978, having been offered the job after a series of demanding interviews, including trial by sherry. At that time, the doctor's wife was a critical member of the team. Often out of hours calls from high profile aristocratic patients came in while the doctor was out, and a cool head and polite voice were required. As Sally was by this stage a senior physiotherapist in intensive case, and came from Woking, these were major advantages. I was taking over from the Senior Partner of more 30 years and some highly important patients were being entrusted to me. The expectation in that day was that once you reached 75, the GP would visit you at home. How things have changed. I was provided with a regular visiting list and noted that after each name were listed such items as "Case of Glenfiddich", "Christmas turkey", or "Brace of Pheasant". "What do these mean?" I asked. The list was hastily retracted and replaced with a simple list of names. I soon realised that all these Christmas "bonuses" had been earned over several years and did not come as a matter of course. I soon managed to get the list trimmed down. After a gentle first 2-week acclimatisation, the surgery and visiting load got busy and the 1 in 3 on-call was tough.

On my first weekend on call, one of our real VIPs (but unknown to me) attended on a Saturday afternoon after an incident with a chain saw that that flown off and badly slashed his neck. In those times, patients rushed to the surgery with all sorts of emergencies, even heart attacks. He was holding a large towel around his neck and making it clear that he had a strong aversion to hospitals. As I removed the towel, it was clear that the damage was extensive, but he seemed to have avoided major arteries and nerves. Having recently worked in a major A and E unit, I cracked on, matched up all the loose tissue and was very pleased with the final result. I applied a dressing and sent him home. Five days later, I was called in by one of the other partners, who was astounded that I had attempted such a complex repair. The bottom line was that the patient was delighted. I learned that he produced limited addition pottery that was in high demand. I was given a piece, which I still have to this day.

The early days of visiting were very tricky at I had little idea where I was going. Often directions were passed on second hand, via Sally, if I was out on another call. This was, of course, long before the age of satellite navigation. One such set of challenging directions at night was, to" the Hollies farm, halfway down the long drive. There is no name on the gate, not sure what colour the gate is, but it used to be painted brown. You can't miss it!". There were many wild goose chases.

On January 3rd, 1979, a call came from Sally, whilst I was out on another call. The message was that Mrs Sproston was having "trouble down below". I found the house and was greeted by a moderately confused elderly gentleman with bilateral hearing aids that seemed to be switched off. "Mrs Sproston, trouble down below", I said. I pushed past him as I could see an old lady in the corner. Mrs S was equally deaf, so I decided to circumvent the story by rolling her over to get a good look. As I was peering up his wife's nether regions, the old boy asked, "And who might you be young man?" "I'm the doctor", I replied. He looked relieved and slightly surprised. I suspected that they might have been waiting in for the gas man.

On 17th January 1979, Sally had handed me an address for an evening visit for Mrs Doris Twemlow at, what looked like, 16 Manor Lane. Of course, most night visits were made with no reference to any notes. The message said, "stomach pains". It was around 11pm that I arrived at the house. The husband greeted me at the door and showed me upstairs. The lady seemed pleased to see me and told me, at some length, about her pains. It seemed like long standing chronic diverticulitis, and it was looking like a bit of a wasted visit. As the new doctor, I was very keen to make a good impression and not upset anybody, so I made reassuring tones and moved towards the door. Only at this point did she say, "It is very nice of you to visit, but we didn't call a doctor". To avoid appearing foolish, I mumbled something about, "Conducting routine home checks and all part of the service!".

I glanced down at the paper and noted that the writing most probably said 18 Manor Lane. I shot out the door, and next door to number 18. The man at number 16 watched me and seemed very impressed that the new young doctor was working his way along the entire street one house at a time at 11pm. Of course, Mrs T was in severe pain and required admission. I apologised for the delay in getting there.

During a busy morning surgery, a week later, I was called to an emergency at a private girls' boarding school as the violin teacher was short of breath. As I started to examine her, the head mistress chipped in with, "She has always been highly strung". Luckily, it was only a panic attack and she settled after rebreathing from a paper bag.

On February 24th, 1979 at 11pm, I was on call again with an address that I had taken down as being 42 Cedar Avenue, with the message, "pains in chest, please use rear entrance (!), door open, patient in bed upstairs". Unfortunately, there was also a Cedar Crescent, and I was headed for the wrong address. Luckily, I was very adept at using the rear entrance. I opened the door, and entered the kitchen, only to be jumped upon by a large man who pinned me to the ground, as his equally large dog sank its teeth into my leg. This time, the "I'm the doctor" story did not seem adequate to get me out of trouble. I was learning the hard way to be more careful checking names and address, particularly over the telephone.

The first 12 months in general practice was tough, especially with having to work up to parity in 3 years. Sally had to give up her job in London and we had insufficient income between us to get a mortgage in an area where housing and rents were expensive. Eventually, at age 30, I was able to get a 2-bedroomed bungalow and Sally had a physio job in Intensive Therapy Unit at North Staffordshire Infirmary. At one stage, the partners had paid themselves back some money that was owed, meaning that for one quarter I received nothing. We were quite low at that stage, wondering if I had made the right decision. I applied for a job as a GP in Saudi Arabia and was successful. We hoped that we might be able to put something aside for the future. Unfortunately, Sally could not get a job in Saudi, meaning that we could not go. On reflection, this was a blessing as life for a woman in Saudi at that stage would have been very restrictive.

I was approached by another practice looking for a new partner, promising me a better deal, but on looking at it in some detail, they were also seeking to exploit the situation for the first 3 years. Nowadays, contracts with long periods to parity are unacceptable and I made sure that new partners in future did not have to go through the same experience. I remember when I eventually sold the bungalow, the estate agent described the garden as "A fine example of deferred maintenance." I stuck it out with the practice, and I was glad I did. I bought the second house at auction, not an experience I would be keen to repeat.

By January 1980, I had sorted out my own list of home visits, on the basis of need, rather than future Christmas presents. I did regularly visit an old lady called Gladys, who was disabled and housebound but insisted on her daughter getting in some fish and chips whenever I was coming. They would be by the fire to keep them warm and we would have a nice chat. Gladys had a heart of gold, but life had not been kind to her. I frequently got into trouble from Sally if I did not devour my lunch. She knew at once if I had visited Gladys for haddock and chips.

It was July 1980, and I had been looking after George Brown, aged 75, who lost his wife 3 years earlier and now lived with his son. He was getting worse and had taken to his bed. His main complaints were tiredness and lack of motivation, but blood tests had been normal, and I concluded that he was probably depressed. I commenced one antidepressant, increased the dose, and prescribed a second one. I was having to visit every few days at his son's request. I approached the local psychiatrist, Dr Patel for a domiciliary visit and we arranged to meet at the house. The son greeted us, and we went upstairs. I entered the room and Mr Brown seemed asleep. I shook him, saying, "Mr Brown, I've brought a specialist, Dr Patel to see you, Mr Brown, Mr Brown". It was now clear that he was dead. His son casually leaned forward, and calmly delivered the statement, "I guess that the depression must have been more severe than you thought, doctor!"

Around the same time, I was having similar problems with Mrs Scraggins, aged 85. She was having dizzy spells and passing out and there seemed to be no obvious reason. I had visited 3-4 times, taken blood tests, and seemed to be getting nowhere. Each time her daughter was present and seemed very attentive. I decided to sit down and discuss the situation, but the daughter and her husband had the only other chairs, so I opted for a pouffe. As I sat down, I spotted the daughter gasp, as I collapsed on the floor midst hundreds of sherry bottles stacked under a throw and made to look like a pouffe. Mrs S would ask all her carers to just get her some eggs... and perhaps a wee sherry, then the next one, just a loaf of bread... and perhaps a wee sherry. The daughter had clearly piled all these bottles knowing exactly what her mother was doing whilst watching the new doctor blunder along trying to find a cause.

In December 1980, I was approached by the local ambulance service to provide emergency cover for the M6 motorway in the event of major accidents. As I was the youngest partner with recent accident and emergency experience, the practice felt that this was a great idea. Little did I realise the implications. As well as my normal practice on-call cover, I was now expected to be available 24/7 to cover on of the major accident blackspots in the country between junctions 17 and 19 of the M6, and with zero payment. I was then informed that no additional equipment was provided, the suggestion being that I might "procure" the necessary medical supplies from the local casualty department. Three weeks into the job, my phone went at 2am on a very cold, foggy night and I was on my way to an incident a mile south on junction 18 of the M6. Although the road was closed, my blue flashing light got me to the scene. What I witnessed could only be described as surreal carnage (my 2 least favourite clichés in one sentence). Armed with my 4 dressing packs and 2 bottles of intravenous fluids, I felt virtually useless in the wake of the incessant screams for help echoing out of the still icy mist. Bodies were strewn by the roadside as rescue workers cut bodies from the wreckage. My only significant contribution was to certify 8 people dead. It was straight on to morning surgery at 8am and I remember not being especially interested in sore throats and verrucae that morning. I recall having flashbacks for some time and wondered if I suffered an element of PTSD. I decided that nights like this were not for amateurs and promptly resigned by post, using practice workload as an excuse. Thankfully, the cover for such events is much more professional nowadays. The major learning experience from this was not to accept posts purely on the basis of feeling flattered.

It was March 1981, and I was back looking for country farmhouse in the dark at 11pm. This was Sharon White, aged 36, wife of a local businessman. She was complaining of right sided abdominal pain. The house had been beautifully renovated, and the message was that she was in bed upstairs and I should let myself in. Her husband was away on a shooting trip. She commented that he was rarely home nowadays, and preferred shooting trips with his friends. Things were not especially good between them, as he was jealous and, at times dominating. The history was a little concerning, there had been difficulty conceiving in the past with a number of infections. She had given up on getting pregnant but was now 3 weeks late but had a few spots of bleeding, and now a pain on the right side, that was getting worse. These symptoms caused me some concern, and I was suspicious of ectopic pregnancy. She suddenly said, "I expect now you'll need to examine me" and threw off the duvet. She was completely naked. Rather than try to rescue the duvet from the floor I decided to carry on examining her abdomen. I informed her that I will need to do an internal examination. Just at the crucial stage of the bimanual assessment, the bedroom door burst open, and there was her husband with a shotgun in his hand. He looked at me, and I look at him and time seemed to stand still. My first thoughts were "Is this the way it ends for me, shot dead by a jealous husband, whilst caught in the act?" and the only pathetic explanation I could think of was "I'm the doctor!" It did turn out to be an ectopic pregnancy and she required surgery to remove the tube and ovary, which would have not been good for future fertility.

This case made me think of the insistence that many doctors have for chaperones. Of course, nothing could have been done here, as I had no idea what I was walking into. As a country GP on call, there just were not random chaperones around waiting for a call. I have never really worried about the issue and feel that needing to ask suggested a feeling of distrust. The patient might think "why does he need someone else here?" It seems to be normal for a female doctor to get a female chaperone, meaning that a poor guy has 2 women ogling his bits. On the other hand, for a female patient, a male doctor and a male chaperone would seem unusual. Perhaps the most vulnerable situation might be a male doctor conducting an intimate examination on a gay patient? Would he want a male chaperone? Randomly available male health care professional chaperones are a rare breed in general practice. What happens if you do not know his orientation? The bottom line for me is that I have had no issues in 40 years and intend to continue that way.

When I arrived in the practice, there were no female partners and I was the one with all the gynaecology experience, especially contraception and IUCD insertion. These were lucrative sources of income for the practice. We soon had female registrars and once I had trained them, I would lose most of the patients, suggesting that the gender of the doctor was far more important than clinical experience.

This brings we to my next case. Mrs Mandy Till, 35, was a checkout attendant at the village supermarket and a regular patient of mine in the contraceptive clinic. I rarely shopped in the village, but this time had popped in for some vegetables on the way back from evening surgery. It was quite busy, with a queue behind me and Mandy was working flat out. Just as she had her hand ready to scan my particularly large cucumber, she suddenly looked up and said “Oh, Dr Hackett, that nasty vaginal discharge still hasn’t cleared up”. Three customers behind me immediately moved to an adjacent checkout.

Sometimes in surgery things slip out of the mouth unintentionally. In January 1984, Mrs Hooper had come to see me with recurrent cystitis and had been awaiting the results of her most recent urine test. “Well doctor, what have we found?” she asked. I looked at the lab report and confidently announced “There is no sign of active infection, but you have multiple *orgasms*". "Really", she said, "and you can tell that from a urine sample, that's amazing". I had to hastily explain the significance of multiple *organisms* in the urine.

A month later, Mrs Nesbit was in the surgery with her 14-year-old daughter, Phoebe, a nervous girl with bothersome asthma. Conscious of her anxiety, I was trying to make her feel relaxed. As she lifted her top and I put the stethoscope to her chest, I said "Now Phoebe, big *breasts*". "Pardon doctor", said the mother. There was really no way back from that one. The more you think that you must not say something, the more likely is to slip out.

Some patients have some names that make it impossible to focus when they come in. I remember Mrs Ivy Dick, who was always bringing her son into the surgery and usually commenced the conversation with "I'm very worried about Everard". Then there was a South African Chap, who played for the village cricket team with me, called George Shaw-Twilly. There are just some names that should not be hyphenated.

It was back on call, and sometimes with holidays, it could be 5 nights on duty on the trot. I had been up most of the night before with a delusional schizophrenic who had to be sectioned. I waited 3 hours at the house for a psychiatric social worker to arrive and sign the form. At 3 am the phone went, and it was Mrs Bacon ringing about her daughter Megan, 16, with stomach pains. This sounded like another wasted trip. I had seen a man 2 nights earlier, rolling in pain. Just after I got there, he let out a huge fart and said, "Ah, better out than in"- problem solved. As I left the house, Sally mumbled, "I bet she's in labour". Megan was a very large girl, and mother told me that she had been to the surgery twice in the last 2 weeks and been given 2 different laxatives. A quick look at her abdomen gave me the diagnosis that she was indeed, in labour. I told Mum to make a cup of tea and sit herself down as I broke the news. "Our Megan's not got herself into trouble has she?" I explained that it had gone a bit further than that. It continues to amaze me how a young girl can get to full term without her or the mother noticing and how 2 doctors could miss a full-term uterus. Megan required a Caesarean Section, but both mother and baby did well afterwards.

I had passed my MRCGP parts 1 and 2 first time in 1980, despite my previous problems with multiple choice. I was working as a research fellow in General Practice in Liverpool, when in 1985, another opportunity presented itself. My father had been out to Brisbane and had been diagnosed with a malignant melanoma on his back whilst seeing a GP for a chest infection. The GP was a family friend of my uncle Tom and it seemed that this doctor, was looking for a GP exchange in the UK, meaning a swap of jobs, houses, cars, pets, everything except wives. As we had a child of 2, with a second on the way, this looked possible and I thought that it was probably now or never. As I still had an Australian passport, it was straight forward and so an exchange was agreed for June 1986 for 4 months. In the back of my mind was the possibility that, if all worked well, we might settle in Australia, as it would be much easier with very young children.

In September 1985, we returned from holiday in Spain to discover that we had been burgled. Luckily, some friends had tidied the place up as it had been badly trashed. Those of us who have been through the experience know how devastating it is. Six months before, I had gone into my garden at lunchtime and interrupted burglars smashing through the patio doors of my next-door neighbours. My chance return home on the day saved them from a similar experience. It was straight back to work after the burglary, and I found myself visiting a 32-year-old woman on one of the estates. She was a regular at the surgery. She suffered with panic attacks and the prescribed tablets were not working. I sat there for some time, delving into her domestic situation. Her partner had been violent and manipulative, but she put this down to the great stress he was under, working all hours, especially nights. "What line is he in?", I asked. "He's a burglar", she answered with not a semblance of shame. I could not believe that, for the last 30 minutes, I had been sympathising with a woman over her partner's stressful life as burglar. He was even possibly the one who had trashed my home. Shortly after this, another partner was burgled and I remembered walking into the waiting room to hear a receptionist, in full range of about 30 people, announcing "Yes, Dr H is away for 2 weeks, with his family and won't he back until February 27th". I suggested that these "friendly family doctor" announcements needed to stop, or that the staff should add that "Dr H will be leaving his 4 Rottweilers in the house and they are all fully trained to extinguish fires".

In June 1986, we set out for Australia with 2 small children on a "round the world" ticket via, Vancouver, Hawaii, and Fiji, arriving in Brisbane. We` stayed in an old colonial house in the suburbs and my practice was in the Stafford district of Brisbane. Before starting work, I had to go before the Queensland Medical Board for a medical licence and had been studying the Australian Healthcare System. As I entered the examination, 3 doctors were trying out a new putter on the carpet. Once they realised that I played golf, the remainder of the assessment consisted of a discussion of relative benefits of a saw grip versus the longer handle.

My first patient in Australia was my uncle Tom, who had come to discuss the results of his recent chest x-ray. I put the x-ray up on the screen and to my horror, it showed a moderately sized lung cancer. What a start! Uncle Tom survived my time there but died shortly afterwards.

My lasting impression was that the Australians did not tolerate waiting lists. Blood tests were done immediately with results were back the same day. The same went for relatively complicated radiology, along with immediate reports. Consultant referrals were usually seen within a matter of days with admissions within a few weeks, even for routine conditions. GPs could earn a lot of money dealing with various forms of skin cancer. Payments for minor operations were related to the number of sutures. I became quite adept in squeezing in the maximum number whenever possible. Virtually every patient would have some form of facial skin damage justifying biopsy, excision, or cryotherapy.

Although we enjoyed the trip, from the outset there was no real chance that we would stay. Although there were some good points about the system as it allowed for a basic "Medicare" system that ensured a good level of basic care, it allowed individuals to "top-up." This meant that the patient could pay to get a better room in the hospital or a GP practice allowing longer consultation. There was also a "Gold Card" service for war veterans, providing higher allowances. I felt that the UK could learn from the Australian system as we do not treat ex-forces personnel particularly well. Overall, I felt that we had more "clinical freedom" in the UK, especially with prescribing. Little did I know how much that would change in the forthcoming years. We returned via Singapore and Bangkok and resumed life in Holmes Chapel in November 1986.

I have often heard doctors say that patients never really appreciate when a doctor has done a good job. You can get things badly wrong, but if you do it with a smile, the patient will think you are great. In contrast, you can make a life-saving diagnosis, but if you come across as slightly arrogant, they will not have a good thing to say about you. The following case demonstrates this:

It was January 1987, and it was another emergency call to a lady, Rose Gordon, 65, at a remote farm. I was following some vague directions once again, but I was pretty confident where it was. I arrived to find a very distressed lady with chest pain, shortness of breath and a very rapid heart rate. After contacting an ambulance, but knowing it would be some time, I rapidly inserted an intravenous line and performed an electrocardiogram (ECG), which showed very fast atrial flutter. For certain she was going to die unless I acted quickly. I remembered that I possibly had the right drug in my bag but realised that things were disorganised as I had not had the chance to check it since returning from Australia. I found the 4 ampoules of verapamil that I was looking for. I administered the first slowly into the vein and noted very little effect, so a few minutes later, 2 more and the rate slowed significantly. Instantly she seemed to improve, and she squeezed my hands in gratitude. I slowly gave the 4th ampoule and the rate was now down virtually to normal. At this point, the ambulance arrived, and the look on the face of the ambulance man displayed the fact that the patient did not look as bad as expected. “Where is the hospital letter?” he said, disapprovingly. Clearly, I should have had my fountain pen out for an elegant referral letter, whist resuscitating the patient. I apologised, and hastily jotted down a list of events as they carried her out to the ambulance. I went home, now wide awake as I could never sleep again after the adrenaline rush of cases like this. Three days later, I noted the husband on my surgery list. I had contacted the hospital in the meantime to confirm that Rose was doing well. Her husband entered the room. I was getting ready for an emotional display of gratitude, wondering where he was hiding the whisky, when he erupted "What have you got to say about this?", thumbing an empty ampoule down on the table. I picked it up. Was he complaining about my lack of tidiness as I had missed an ampoule amidst all the chaos? "It's 3 months out of date". He shouted. He left the consultation in no doubt that his wife would have died without this drug and he was very lucky to find a GP who carried a selection of cardiac drugs. From that day on, I was meticulous about checking the dates on the drugs in my bag, well for a year or so anyway. This became an issue a few years later when we began to carry "clot buster" drugs costing several hundred pounds, only for the majority to be discarded when out of date.

Such experiences persuaded us to carry a defibrillator when on-call. Often when you might have needed it for an emergency, it would be the boot of a partner's car at the golf club, but on one occasion I had it with me and leapt into action. The patient was a huge man who had passed out on his bed with no sign of a cardiac output. Everything was good to go, and I was just about to discharge, when I noticed that 4 family members were holding onto the metal bed frame, having failed to realise what the words, "stand back" meant. I was remarkably close to recording a score of *minus five* for a cardiac resuscitation.

General Practice is often defined as an art and not a science. As a junior hospital doctor, we would tick every box on the blood form and order every x-ray possible on the basis that something will turn up. Primary Care would be impossible if we all did this and the NHS would be bankrupted. We therefore had to rely on a "sixth sense" that something was not right. The following two cases demonstrate this.

Jennifer was 21 months and had presented with reluctance to put her foot to the ground. There was little to find on examination, and the case had all the features of a difficult child playing up to anxious parents. I arranged an x-ray of the entire leg, which was normal, and I could see that the parents were just beginning to get slightly frustrated with me. After listening to the mother for some time, I began to realise that, perhaps, all was not right here. I picked up the phone and spoke to one of the paediatricians, who saw her that day. Jennifer had a nasty form of leukaemia. For the next 2 years Jennifer and her family bravely fought the disease, but she sadly died. During that time, I became very close to the family and to this lovely little girl. Sadly, as so often happens, it also took its toll on the parents' marriage.

The second case was Bethan, a baby of 6 weeks brought to a Saturday morning surgery with feeding problems and being sick after most but not all milk feeds. Now, there are several cases presenting like this in the average GPs day. I gave the usual advice and suggested some infant Gaviscon and moved on. For some reason, later the Saturday afternoon, I was doing a home visit in the same village and found myself going past the house. It was a lovely day and work was slow. For some reason, call it "sixth sense", I pulled into the drive and knocked on the door. It was feeding time, and I walked into the lounge to see Bethan produce a projectile vomit of about 3 metres. The diagnosis of pyloric stenosis was immediately clear. I could feel a tight band of muscle at the lower end of the stomach. This can only be effectively treated by surgery. Bethan was admitted, had the operation, and thrived from then on. Unfortunately, many parents have picked up on the term "projectile vomiting" and use it routinely to impress. There is no doubt when you see a proper case.

One of the toughest tasks in general practice is managing patients who clearly need an operation but need to wait on long waiting lists. Some waited for years, especially if an orthopaedic surgeon has told them to "Go away and lose 5 stones". Such a woman was Olive Green, 75, suffering terrible pain from her right hip. She had already waited 9 months and still had not been seen in clinic. At that stage, I was regularly going to Old Trafford with the Manchester United Consultant, who had carried out hip and knee surgery on high profile sportsmen. I told her that I would "call in a favour" and get her seen sooner. She seemed extremely pleased. I rang the surgeon that evening and he replied, "Seeing as It's you, I will fit her in at the end of clinic tomorrow". Unfortunately, helping a mate is totally out of the question in the modern NHS. I rang Olive with the news that evening. There was a long pause on the phone. I assumed that she might have been overcome with relief. After a few seconds she replied, "Your chap can't be very good if he can see me tomorrow, I think I'll stick with the original specialist".

On Monday 28th January 1988, I was last to finish surgery and found that I had been allocated an emergency call for a 52-year old with a bad back at the "Sun and Air Naturist Colony", at Allostock, near Knutsford. The practice manager felt, for some reason, that I was best equipped to handle the case. When I arrived at the gate, the attendant insisted that I would need to remove my clothes before entering, but I would be allowed to wear my stethoscope. As one, who has fortunately not required the services of the "Small Penis Clinic" at Sheffield, this caused me only slight concern. I asked where I should put my thermometer. Luckily, he could not keep the joke up any longer and let me in fully clothed. It was quite daunting, wandering around this large campsite, being the only person wearing clothes. As the tents were not well numbered, I was slightly flustered by the time I got to the correct one, having disturbed several naturist couples during their afternoon naps. There was little room in the tiny tent for a proper examination, and I remember conducting straight leg raising on the grass, exposing this gent's testicles to all passers- by. As I left, it was getting a bit nippy any I found it strange that the naturists chose to wear a jacket to keep warm whilst leaving the bottom half uncovered. I must have gone down well as the manager of the site rang the practice later to informed them that I had all the necessary credentials to be their regular doctor. Subsequently I visited a few more times, but I have never fully embraced the naturist philosophy, especially in winter in Northern England.

I managed my entire GP career without a formal complaint from a patient. I am convinced that the key was never to "lecture" patients or "patronise" them. I believe that whenever you do so, that patient "marks your card", such that the next time that your management falls short, that patient will probably complain. The nearest I came to a complaint was in my weekly session in occupational health at the local hospital. A man had travelled up from Cardiff for a medical in relation to a possible job. Our excellent nurse had uncovered some poor performance issues and a pattern of drug abuse leading us to a decision to fail him on medical grounds. On this day, I had brought my 3-month Labrador, Lucy, into the clinic as Sally was working, and Jean, the clinic nurse, wanted to see the puppy. Not only was the gentleman not happy at coming all that way, only to fail a medical but he realised that my Labrador had sneaked into his changing cubicle and eaten his socks. We knew this as one had been regurgitated on the clinic floor. I remember suggesting that the good news was that his “lab tests” were all normal, but he did not see the joke. He looked a sorry sight walking away down the corridor with bare ankles showing above his shoes, a fashion statement well ahead of his time. The second sock appeared a few days later on our kitchen floor. Lucy bit off more than she could chew when she ate my lucky underpants. They had to be removed surgically by the vet and never quite fitted as snugly from that day onwards.

In April 1990, I was invited to be doctor for the making of the Robin Hood movie filmed at Peckforten Castle in Cheshire. Unfortunately, this was not the “Hollywood style” Kevin Costner version but a more traditional version starring Patrick Bergin, Uma Thurman, and Edward Fox. Although it might sound glamourous, the work mainly involved a few of the Sheriff’s men with bad backs and the after effects of Mead and Wenching orgies. Although I did not get official recognition, I did make an unscripted entry stage right in one of the fight scenes. It might be worth getting a copy from the archives now that “Blockbuster” is no more. Blink twice and you will miss my brief entry. I do not think it made the “Directors Cut”.

In June 1990, there was a case that still haunts me today. I was called late at night by a mother, who I knew to be a nurse at the local learning disability unit. Her 3-year-old had a temperature and cough. I visited at around mid-night and diagnosed a simple viral illness, avoiding an antibiotic as the practice pharmacist had commented that I had the highest prescribing rate, a badge of shame. The mother was clearly struggling to cope, but who wouldn't with a 3-year-old and a small baby? I noticed a cot and asked about the infant, who I believed to be 12 weeks. I remembered the mother from a couple of years before I had switched her to a" mini-pill". She made the strange comment, "Can I sue you if it fails?" The following morning, I was on my way to Keele University and would be going past the house. I promised to drop in and check on the child. When I arrived, the 3-year-old was better, but sleeping, and the baby boy had been placed on the chair whilst mother answered the door. I played with him, tickled his tummy, and made him chuckle. He was the picture of health. Later in the day I returned for evening surgery to learn that, at 10.30 that morning, one of my partners was called out as the baby was found dead by the mother. My partner diagnosed a cot death syndrome. I was totally shocked. I did not visit the mother afterwards, as she had taken a liking to one of the female partners. I next saw the mother 12 months later about a minor matter and I asked how she and her family were coping. She was now active in the "Sudden Infant Death Association" offering counselling to other parents. She suddenly looked me in the eye and said, "You don't know, do you?". I asked what he meant and after a few seconds hesitation, she said "Never mind". I wonder to this day why she came to check what I knew or suspected and what she was might have been close to telling me.

Many GPs will recognise the “Absent Relative Syndrome”, a familiar occurrence on bank holiday weekends. In this case, it was August Bank holiday in 1990. This usually involves a long-time absent son or daughter, often a “high-flier”, who decides to visit Mum or Dad, after an absence of several years. In this case, 80-year-old Reginald, with terminal cancer of the pancreas was being looked after at home by Maud, 80, assisted by the practice nurse. This was well before the days of regular visits from McMillan nurses and shared hospice care. My partner had been visiting at least once daily and was administering regular morphine injections to keep him comfortable. A naso-gastric tube was helping Maud to get some fluids down. Reginald’s son, an investment banker from London had visited on the bank holiday Saturday and was shocked to see the decline in his father, from a year earlier when he last visited. He decided that things needed to be “sorted” and he demanded an urgent visit from the duty doctor. I arrived to find Reginald clearly distressed with a “bubbling chest” and a matter of hours to live. I sat the son and his wife down and gave them a long explanation of the extent of the cancer and how the palliative care programme was working. I stated that I would give him a further injection to relieve his distress and return that evening. I told them to prepare for the worst and that we were looking at hours rather than days. I thought that the son had taken all of this in when suddenly he announced, “Would it make a difference if we went privately?”

A few weeks later, I was called to Hilda, 90, who was in the late stages of palliative care for cancer of the oesophagus. She had long since been unable to swallow and nutrition was provided with liquids through a narrow tube inserted into her stomach. Although Hilda was unconscious, brewing a terminal pneumonia, husband, Ron, was trying to crush her statin tablets and blood pressure tablets and force them down the tube, but now the tube was blocked. I explained to the family that Hilda had a matter of hours to live and that treating her cholesterol and blood pressure was now pointless. I advised that they stop the tablets and I unblocked the tube. Hilda's daughter, visiting from Surrey, then announced, "The heart specialist said that she must *always* take these tablets otherwise something serious, like a heart attack or stroke might happen". I attempted to explain that something a lot more serious than that had happened and completely changed the circumstances. I later learned that one of my partners was called back later that evening and restarted the cholesterol and blood pressure tablets. Hilda died relatively comfortably the next morning.

In August 1991, I was late arriving back for evening surgery pulled into my parking place and headed for the front door. Out of the corner of my eye, I noted a Ford Fiesta, performing some elaborate manoeuvres in the car park, when to my horror, I spotted that he seemed to be reversing into the "doctors" bay where I had just parked. I noted the car was driven by an elderly gentleman, who was looking straight ahead as he reversed. I shouted loudly, but he continued, crashing into the rear of my car. He got out of the car and inspected the damage. I politely asked why he was not looking and why he had not responded to my shouting. "Terrible arthritis in the neck and deaf as a post nowadays", he replied. Not much you can say about that. He then turned to me and said, "I must say that you're taking this much better than most people I crash into". He then produced the card of his preferred garage, saying £450 should just about cover it. Ultimately his estimate was within £10 of the final price. I excused myself, as I was late, and 5 minutes later, I was starting my surgery with an elderly driving medical assessment, a great chance to catch up on time. “Mr Reginald Molehusband”, I called. Who should appear, but the man from the car park incident? He explained that he only used the car for local shopping and to pop out to the doctor or pharmacy, for prescriptions for his housebound wife, Maud. Reginald, 89, was unsteady, totally unable to turn his neck without going dizzy, deaf, and failed the eyesight test miserably. Despite these findings and the earlier events, he seemed totally surprised and devastated when I broke the news that he had failed the medical.

In September 1991, I was approached by a rich businessman, MN, from Pakistan, who had recently moved to a mansion in the area. He had a much younger English wife, who had been a very promising tennis player, who had appeared at Junior Wimbledon. He had selected me to look after both of them, including his newly pregnant wife’s maternity care. He seemed charming and made some generous donations to the practice over the next few months. They took Sally and I out to restaurants, such as La Belle Epoque in Knutsford, not normally affordable for us. All went well, and a successful delivery of a baby girl resulted in even more donations. I was on duty, on the August bank holiday in 1992, when I was called out at 2 am in the morning on the Saturday, as the baby had a high temperature. The father was wearing a silk dressing gown and their master bedroom was magnificent. As the baby vomited all down the front of his gown, I thought to myself that life was a great leveller. I diagnosed an ear infection, prescribed an antibiotic, and promised to look back in the morning. The baby was much better when I checked at 10 am in the morning. In the daylight, I was impressed by the magnificence of the estate. He had his own landing strip and I spotted at least 2 planes on the runway. I was also struck by the tight security. I wondered how anybody could have made so much money by the age of 40.

The rest of the weekend was hectic and on the Bank Holiday Monday morning, the morning papers arrived, and I collected them as I took Sally her usual breakfast in bed. The front pages all had coverage of a huge undercover police raid on the mansion of a Cheshire millionaire, exposed as a major drug dealer and fraudster. They had acted on a tip-off that a major consignment was arriving in the middle of the night via his private airstrip. I certainly had my answer as to how he was that rich by 40. The extent of his corruption was revealed over several pages. He received 15 years and, of course, lost his wife and daughter. I later realised that MN was released after 9 years but was killed shortly afterwards flying a light aircraft. There was a strong suspicion of suicide. The mansion was purchased by a former Aston Villa and England footballer, who subsequently played for Manchester City, Everton, and West Bromwich Albion. At the current time, it is on the market at £4.2 million.

By 1992, I was finding things tough. One partner had been off long-term sick and the out of hours was stressful, often 5 days on call 24/7. I was also faced with 2 sets of private school fees with a third to follow. I was doing routine visits in the evening simply because there had been no free time in the day. Sometimes I was having to wake the patient for a visit they were expecting earlier in the day. Administrative meetings dominated and we had become heavily involved in fundholding. We had taken on a finance manager and a decision had been made to negotiate packages with different hospitals to save money. I was never happy with the concept of fundholding, with practices making money by restructuring referrals. Of course, the concept was dismantled by the Labour government 2 years later.

I was also developing my interest in sexual medicine after my "Road to Damascus" moment with Mr Mike Heal at Leighton Hospital, when I discovered that we had the power to restore a man's erections. I had tried to treat some patients in my surgery but was told that "The receptionists were concerned about what you were doing with these men behind closed doors" and that "This must stop and you should send them to the psychiatrists where they belong". I was now working for a private clinic at weekends and was seeing the great possibilities that we now had to treat these men. The final straw was Sally calling me in and saying "Geoff, may I introduce you to your 2-year-old son, Dan?" Things had to change". It was now clear by 1993 that I needed to make some major life changing decisions.

The 6 months that followed my decision to move on were very difficult. Essentially, I did my own surgeries and drank coffee and had lunch in my own room with little contact with the other doctors. At age 42, making the right move was not straight forward. There was certainly no "head-hunting" in general practice. Luckily, I spotted a potential job in Lichfield, about 50 miles away, but equidistant with Keele University where I was working as a Senior Lecturer. I was working for an MD in Sexual Problems in Men, which I eventually achieved in 2000. The Lichfield advertisement was for a half-time partner, which would allow me more time to develop my interest in men's health. I later discovered that they were looking for a female partner, to replace one who was leaving. Even at this time advertisements could not be that blatant, so I was shortlisted. A couple of consultants at Leighton Hospital went out of their way to contact the practice to help me. At times like this, you find out who your true friends are. When I attended for interview, I was told that they had several more to see, but on return home, I received a call to say that the job was mine. We even managed to sell our house in Cheshire and move into a place in the country near Lichfield on the same day I started work. The saving grace was that state schools in Lichfield were much better and we were able to save on long term private education. With the support of Mike Heal and a business plan to run a "stand-alone service" I convinced Good Hope Hospital, Sutton Coldfield that an ED clinic was needed. The good news was that I would be starting with the title "Consultant in Urology" as I already held a post as University senior lecturer. Things fell into place very quickly and I started on 1st July 1993.

There were other excellent benefits from the move. The new practice looked after a GP maternity unit, with GP beds in the community hospital, where out of hours patients were also seen, with the assistance of trained minor injuries nurses. We were also responsible for the local hospice and renal unit. The work was varied, challenging, and rewarding and I had escaped all the ethical issues around fundholding.

A major benefit of the re-location was that a surgeon and old friend from Crewe, John Clegg, exerted family influence in order to secure membership for me at Little Aston Golf Club, in Sutton Coldfield. Previously, I had been at Mere Golf and Country Club in Knutsford, where a gold medallion and chest wig were almost standard attire. Now I had arrived at a proper "gentleman's club". I invited a Sandbach GP and old friend, Mike Olver, for a game at my new club and he immediately fell afoul of the compulsory "jacket and tie" rule. After a rush of protestations from members, the formidable steward, Bob, presented him a green and red striped blazer, size 52 chest, with a pink and yellow spotted "kipper" tie, specially designed for such occasions. Suitably chastened by the experience, Mike and I had a great game and returned for a hot shower. On exiting the shower, Mike asked where the towels were. "The end door on the right" I explained. A minute or so later, I realised that he had taken the door on the left, which led straight into the main bar, which was packed with members. It seemed like about 5 minutes before he returned, stark naked. He commented that not a single member in the bar mentioned the dress-code and, in fact, 2 guys had suggested that he was exactly the type of new member the club needed.

Undaunted by this experience, I put forward another friend, Andy, for membership. As was the protocol, he attended for his "trial round" with the Tsar and 2 committee members. All seemed to be going well for him, when, as he was coming down the last hole, a wild shot struck by a local GP, Peter G, came over the trees and struck Andy squarely in the R testicle. We carried him off the course and he felt that a warm shower might ease the pain, as the swelling was now considerable. At this stage, Peter G arrived in the clubhouse and we explained what has happened. "Where is the poor chap?" the GP said, and we pointed to the showers. As Andy was washing his hair, he became aware that a hand had appeared between the shower curtains and was palpating his right testicle. He remained motionless until the hand had moved on. As he later told us of this encounter, I asked whether he had found the experience "somewhat strange". He replied, "I just thought that it was part of the initiation ceremony!" He must have passed with flying colours as he was fast tracked to Captain and subsequently long- term treasurer.

One of my earliest on-call experiences in the new practice came in September 1993, when I had to attend the death of a 3-year-old who had been tragically strangled by a cord on some lounge curtains simply by slipping off a chair. It was incredible to think that such an event could happen because of simple set of lounge curtains.

Soon after this, another night of psychiatric mayhem arrived. I was called to a house on one of the estates where the local police had an emergency situation. I rushed to the address to be met by about a dozen armed police offers with batons and riot shields, gathered in the kitchen of the house. A 23-year-old man, Shaun, which a known psychiatric history had threatened his mother with a large Arabic sword. She had escaped to safety. Shaun was isolated in the lounge with a collection of swords and was threatening anybody who tried to enter. The senior police officer had a cunning plan, "Shaun, we're sending in the doctor", ushering me to the door. Suddenly, I was pushed through the door armed only with a Gladstone bag. I hoped that I had not unknowingly upset him at some stage. While he was distracted by my arrival, the armed police charged him, pinning him to the ground. I wondered whether the police believed that GPs were surrounded by an impermeable force shield or were they simply collateral damage? The rest of the night, until 6am was spent with the emergency psychiatric team, deciding whether to section him. The eventual decision was that, with weapons removed and a regular nurse visit to ensure compliance with medication, then he would be fine.

"We're sending in the doctor."

I always founded dealing with suicide very difficult. In my last practice I had seen 3, all men. I was always struck not only by the lack of warning, but how the victim often plans the visual impact of the scene. Certainly, the memories of these events will remain with me for life. My first was a local undertaker, who dressed in his old military uniform before hanging himself. I remember being asked to visit the house and peeping through the letter box to see his pristine polished military boots suspended in mid-air. The second was an eminent Lord of the Realm, who was facing dishonourable exposure. He opted for minimal dress but impaled himself on his masonic sword in an immaculate white bedroom. The third was also a businessman facing financial ruin, who dressed up in his best pin-striped suit.

On this occasion, it was a 19-year-old, who was brought by the mother, saying that the boy was threatening suicide. The warning sign was that his father had committed suicide 5 years earlier. I tried my best to get the crisis team involved immediately, without success but there was an appointment for a couple of weeks. Three days later, he attended to see a partner, complaining of infected rope burns to the neck and was prescribed antibiotic tablets and cream. This worked beautifully, as a week later, the wounds had healed well enough to complete the job properly, a day before the crisis appointment. Around the same time a local farmer rang me expressing negative thoughts. As I was in the middle of a busy surgery, we fitted in an appointment at the end, but he promptly went to the stable and shot himself in the head.

On the brighter side, in June 2001 came on of my greatest successes. I was on call one weekend and was just visiting a patient of mine on the ward, when I was summoned to the delivery suite where a new-born baby was struggling to breathe. There was a weak pulse, so we cleared the airway and ventilated the baby with oxygen through a mask. It was many years since I had intubated a new-born baby and I did not think it was worth the risk trying now. I took the baby in an ambulance to A and E at Burton Hospital with continual ventilation and repeated suction. I feared the worst when the paediatricians struggled to insert the tube. After a stormy couple of days, the baby did well. It was gratifying that the parents went out of their way to track me down and sent me a card on her birthday for several years. The important learning point here was that this had been classified as a very low risk delivery identified as suitable for a community delivery. In effect there is no such thing as a "no risk" delivery.

In 2003, came my nearest thing to a complaint. It was 10pm one evening and I was called to the roughest area in the practice to a man of 62 with low abdominal pain. The house was badly neglected with minimal lighting. He had been seen by another partner twice and it was unclear what, if any, diagnosis was made. I checked his urine and it contained white cells and blood, so I diagnosed a urine infection and gave him an antibiotic. I was woken at 2 am, as he was now worse. Rather than revisit the house, I called for an ambulance to take him to the GP hospital, arranging a bed for him. I told the ward to ring me when he arrived. The phone went at 5am, as ambulances had been busy that night, so I headed to the GP hospital. Now that I could do a proper examination, it was clear that he had peritonitis and was very sick. I immediately contacted the surgeons. He turned out to have necrotising colitis, so called "flesh eating infection". He lost a large piece of bowel but fortunately survived. Around 6 months later the solicitors letter arrived with all the doctors in the practice named. The report went on "It was only the prompt action of the doctor at the hospital that saved his life". I do not think he had realised that the doctor who visited him at home was also the one at the hospital. When this was pointed out, the case against me was dropped.

By 2005, my NHS clinic, private work and research were growing. I was also doing appraisals and had 2 sessions as Medical Adviser for the Primary Care Trust. It was becoming difficult to fit in a lot of the International travel. I was confident that I was pulling my weight in the practice, but an event was about the change things. Over the years, all the partners had immediately passed all the "men's problems" to the practice "expert", whilst still expecting me to see all the routine stuff. Things were moving away from personalised lists by then anyway. It seemed to surprise the Primary Care Trust (PCT) pharmacists that if one doctor sees 100% of patients with a problem, then they are likely to be a high prescriber for that condition.

There is always much discussion about patients who call out doctors unnecessarily. Every serous debate I have ever heard on the subject fails miserably when a tragic case is raised when a patient died as a result of doctor not visiting. I always tried to visit when requested but sometimes the body was not physically capable. In March 2005, the practice had a problem patient, Millicent Rogers, who had chronic chest disease related to smoking. She was requesting home visits on a daily basis. At the practice meeting, we agreed that requests to visit in future should come through her husband and carer, Roy. I was on call the next evening when I received a call from Millicent requesting a visit, as she could not breathe. She clearly had no trouble speaking on the phone. I asked to speak to Roy, who confirmed that he did not think a visit was necessary. Roy found Millicent dead in bed the next morning.

In May 2005, I was coming to the end of a busy evening surgery when Mr Richard (call me Dick) Cumming arrived. He was concerned about some urinary symptoms and a slightly raised PSA. I concluded that a digital rectal examination was required. I was acknowledged to have the most educated digit in the practice. As he was rambling on a bit, I put him in a side room while I saw another patient. I had been on call all day and was running well behind. I entered the room and Dick started wittering on again. I told him to roll over on his left side, pull down his pants and draw up his knees. At that precise moment, there was a knock on the door, “Dr Hackett, we have an acute emergency, a patient has collapsed in the shopping precinct”. I quickly said to Dick,” Stay right there as you are, until I come back”. I grabbed by bag and shot out the door. The collapsed patient in the precinct came round but seemed to have been out for some time. I had to wait around until she was safely on the ambulance. I returned to the surgery and the receptionist greeted me with the words I wanted to hear “The others have seen your last couple of patients, get yourself home and put your feet up”. An hour later, I was relaxing with a nice glass of wine when the phone went. It was one of the cleaners, who had entered my side room to find Dick still in perfect pose presenting his rectum for digital examination. I was impressed that he had followed my instructions precisely. I returned to the surgery and completed the examination. This case took me back to a story of an elderly senior partner, who had firmly told a patient to remain on complete best rest until he returned. Unfortunately, the GP collapsed and died suddenly a few days later. The woman was found 2 weeks later still in bed waiting for him.

I had been looking after a man with mesothelioma, the worst form of lung cancer, usually due to asbestos exposure. In his last few months, he wanted to be able to make love to his wife and “be a man” for as long as possible. Strictly speaking, this dreadful condition does not make a man eligible for NHS therapy, unless he suffers severe distress! Clearly an imminent nasty death would be severely distressing and putting him on a waiting list for me to refer to myself at the hospital just to make the decision was simply daft. I rang the pharmacist at the PCT, who essentially told me “Rules are rules”. Luckily, I had remembered the reasons I went into medicine, so I gave them a liberal supply of tablets to enjoy what time they had left. They told me something that I have heard many times, that preserving the ability to make love is a vitally important part of terminal care. He burst into tears when he explained what it meant to them. Unfortunately, his wife later came to the clinic for more tablets a few weeks later and another partner refused to prescribe them, stating that he did not qualify and that I had acted in breach of the rules. The woman was in an emotional state and said some very strong words to the other partner. The PCT pharmacist was later asked to perform a detailed search to find other cases where I might have circumvented the regulations by not referring patients to myself.

I remember around this time one of the partners informed me that "I was the greatest patient advocate that he had ever come across". I thanked him, but he replied, "that wasn't a compliment".

After 28 years as a GP Principal, I felt the time had come to be a full-time Sex Tsar.

CHAPTER 8.
The Sex Tsar in Clinical Research

I suppose I was always interested in research. Having a physiotherapist as a wife, I first looked at the impact of employing a physiotherapist in primary care and later showed that this could be cost effective in terms of reduced prescribing of medication and time lost from work. I was awarded 2 prizes for this work. The first was the Charles Oliver Hawthorn award by the BMA in 1986 and the second was the Duke of Edinburgh prize in Sports Medicine in 1992. The latter was awarded by Prince Philip himself at St James's Palace. I remember, having received the prize, accompanied by Sally, we were waiting for Prince Philip to join us for celebratory drinks. His assistant warned Sally that he would go straight for her, clearly based on vast experience. As he entered, it was also as though he was scanning the room…. boring old fart to right, pretty woman left… turn left immediately, and there he was. The rest of us were completely ignored. He had quickly discovered that Sally was a physio and might be interested in his groin strain from an old polo injury. He looked to be guiding her hand in the direction of the royal groin with photographers straining for tomorrow's front page or caption competition for "have I got news for you". In the nick of time, his PA directed him down the line and Sally looked visibly relieved.

My success in Sports Medicine, led to a tentative approach from Manchester United to take over from the current GP, who was retiring after 25 years. I was invited to speak at a Sports Injuries day, attended by Alex Ferguson, staff and several players. My 30-minute talk was the last of the day. I soon realised that I had no chance, coming after 4 orthopaedic surgeons, each armed with 150 slides in 30 minutes. In the end, I had 5 minutes to do myself justice. The club clearly appreciated brevity. When I saw the job description, I realised that the previous GP had done the job for 4 directors box tickets and a bottomless bar bill. Later, I was approached by Aston Villa, and Doug Ellis, chairman at the time, held the decision open until my return from holidays. My enquiries had confirmed my suspicions that "Deadly Doug "did not get his name by accident and expected 24/7 on call. I politely withdrew. In 1996, I got to the last 3 for interview at Edgbaston for the GP job of the England Cricket Tour to India and Sri Lanka, including the World Cup. I was unsuccessful but subsequently found that this turned out to be the most disastrous tour on record with, no wins, and the team doctor and a couple of players returning home after 3 weeks with severe food poisoning. In 2010, I did accept a job as medical adviser to the European Golf Tour, which has proved very flexible and highly rewarding.

By 1987, I had started to work on MD thesis at Keele University, where I had recently been appointed a senior lecturer in general practice. I had begun to cultivate some simple clinical trials on new drugs in the practice. They paid very well in the early years but with time and increased red tape, they become hard work for seemingly less reward.

It was really with the "discovery "of drug induced erection in 1988, that my research direction changed. At Keele University, I linked up with Professor Peter Croft and Dr Kate Dunn, a research fellow at the time, to conduct the largest study to that date, looking at the prevalence of sexual problems in men and women and how they are associated with common medical conditions such as diabetes and high blood pressure. From these publications, I was targeted for the further studies in drugs to improve sexual function. In an earlier chapter, I described the arrival of Alan Riley and the set-up for the first Viagra studies, and it was clear from very early that this drug would change the world. These studies involved patients with ED being allocated to either Viagra or placebo. They would then keep a diary of all the sexual events and our role was to collect and collate the results. In 1993, I had a barn converted as a clinic. Luckily, this was before the days of the Care Quality Commission (CQC), as we had the odd field mouse visiting the surgery, no lift, no designated disabled parking, and no in-house interpreters. Even worse was my 80-year-old father who lived upstairs and was prone to wander down unannounced in his loosely fitting pyjamas.

More trials followed, involving similar drugs, vardenafil and tadalafil and I felt privileged to be part of a golden age for medical research. Each trial involved an investigator's meeting, and a great chance to meet colleagues. At one of the earlier ones in London, the first day of the meeting had gone well, and we were sitting down to the conference dinner afterwards. Dr Bollinger was sitting across the table and I could see signs of the agitated twitch, sweating, and drooping lower lip which could only mean one thing… "corporate chicken with cheap house wine". As usual his phone was out, and a table already booked in a local restaurant. He looked around the table for possible dining companions, and as usual, I got the nod. Four of us went on for a very expensive French meal, preceded by a libation or 3. Then it was on to Dr B's jazz club, where he was warmly embraced by the patron. A magnum of Krug disappeared rather quickly. It must have been 3.30am, when we approached the hotel. He paused and exclaimed "feeling peckish, fancy a little Chinese?" In those days, I felt that I could hold my own, but that night I realised that Dr B was now in a different league. We were back at the hotel just in time for the morning breakfast session of day 2 of the meeting. As always, with Dr B, I never usually contributed to meetings until after the first coffee break.

From 1996 to 2005, there was a steady stream of Erectile Dysfunction trials involving the 3 oral drugs. These were straightforward and it was very easy to recruit patients as there was no other acceptable treatment, and otherwise they would have to pay privately. A major eye opener was the greater frequency of sex in the older couples, often multiple times a day. They frequently asked for additional diaries. Despite this high level of use in trials, the NHS decided to restrict tablets to once per week with no evidence to support the decision. I was also able to divert patients from my NHS clinic, ensuring that they had access to the most current therapies and unlimited medication. Involvement in these trials cemented a role as a Key Opinion Leader leading to invitations to international meetings, the subject of another chapter.

Not all drugs were as successful as sildenafil (Viagra) and tadalafil (Cialis). One pharma company developed a drug called apomorphine (Uprima) which worked differently. Whereas Viagra works by opening the blood vessels leading to the penis, this drug supposedly worked by stimulating the nerve pathways from the brain to the penis. Their key message was "Uniting Mind and Body". The studies had been conducted in the US and they had appointed Dr Bollinger (who else) as their international adviser. Dr B was sceptical of the US data and patient selection and some of us were not seeing these results in the early patients we treated. Dr B came to me with a protocol for a 2-centre study that we could conduct quickly to address these issues. He drew up a contract with the company and we signed up for the study. Within weeks, it was becoming clear to the world that this drug was relatively ineffective, and the company decided to withdraw it. Dr B pointed out that he and I had a contract that needed to be honoured. They had to agree and paid up, meaning that effectively we were paid without seeing a patient – top man Dr B.

The next large potential growth area was Premature Ejaculation (PE). Dr Bollinger had been working with a professor from Belfast and a prominent scientist to develop the "ejaculometer". This was designed as an experimental model to evaluate oral and topical drugs developed to treat Premature ejaculation. PE was defined as less than 2 minutes after penetration, although this was later revised to 1 minute. The ejaculometer was a primitive electrical device consisting of a timer and a stimulating pad that flicked the penis at a standardised frequency until ejaculation resulted. Our role was to use the device on patients to confirm PE and then later to evaluate the response of active medication and placebo. There were a few logistic issues. The patient had to be connected the machine and then, for obvious reasons, the doctor had to start the machine and timer and quickly withdraw from the consulting room. I remember waiting outside the door for one patient, thinking that the machine was rather noisy. I could hear a groaning from the room, and politely enquired, "Everything OK?". "Nearly there……. Ahhhhhh"". I guessed from the sounds that he was now actually there. I gave him suitable time, knocked, and entered the room. The timer read

1 minute 40 seconds, so I confirmed his eligibility for the studies. "I'm not sure where it went", he said, "It just shot out, I looked everywhere". This really was a mystery, but I had further patients to see and had to crack on". Twenty minutes later, I was well on with the next consultation, and felt a large drip on my head. "What was that?" said the patient. Quickly I thought of a response, "Having a bit of trouble with that roof," hoping the patient would not realise that it had not rained in several weeks and we were on the ground floor of a 2 -story building. I wound up the consultation and hastily cleaned up the lampshade. I remember that Sally later asked if I was having a "bad hair day". I often refer to this as my Cameron Diaz moment. We eventually published our results from the ejaculometer study in an aptly named journal supplement "Seminal Contributions".

"Another 30 seconds shoiuld do it."

Dr Bollinger, the Tsar, and several other investigators were soon at a meeting in 2000, for studies of Dapoxetine, a tablet that works on the brain to delay ejaculation. The protocol was being discussed by a prominent world expert from the Netherlands. He explained that, although timing was crucial and relatively straight forward to measure, it could not be the only standard. Satisfaction with the sexual experience was important and there were well validated questionnaires to access this. The final and crucial issue was concept of control. He deliberated, "Now, that's when things start to get really sticky". He was clearly totally unaware of the significant of the statement. These trials were truly fascinating. It was more reliable when the partner used the stopwatch as it reduced the pressure on the man. The downside was that she was now a subject in the study, causing logistic issues.

There were several spin-off trials in the PE programme. There was considerable concern that the female issues in PE were not being addressed as they were unlikely to complain about fear of upsetting her partner. This study involved advertising for couples on local radio to attend the centre. This was going to capture couples with and without PE. Subjects and their partners would be paid to complete confidential questionnaires to detect whether partners of men with PE, were suffering themselves and experiencing distress. As we were essentially paying couples to have sex whilst using a stopwatch, we had hundreds of responders. Among them was an undercover journalist, who rather embellished the standard information that my nurse was reading from the script. The "expose" in the Birmingham Post described us as an "exclusive private clinic", paying couples to have as much sex as possible and in *as many positions as possible.* Although this was described as an "Observational Study", this did not mean that anybody would be watching. This was full page coverage with a picture of a scantily clad couple in a lusty pose underneath the huge headline, BONKERS!

Subsequently we conducted further PE studies involving a local anaesthetic spray, that often made both couples numb such that neither knew if anybody had come. We drew the line on one involving injections of Botox into the penis.

As we were now a first port of call for companies with sexual medications, many other companies came to us. One company had a needle free injection of an ED drug that essentially "blasted" the drug through the skin but left the skin raw and bleeding. One involved an inhaled drug, which was curtailed as some patients dropped blood pressure and fainted. We made the right decision not to be involved in these.

We were approached by one company with a hard sell for an ED drug that involved rubbing a nitrate cream on the penis prior to sex. The principal was that nitrates, used to treat angina, open blood vessels, and increase flow. If applied as a cream, this might promote erection. We first learned of the study when the CEO took Dr Bollinger and the tsar out to dinner at a Michelin star restaurant near Vilamoura in Portugal. He made the major mistake of handing the wine list to Dr B. For some, this had been the final blunder of their careers. When the bill arrived, I saw the chap's knees buckle under the shock.

At the investigator meeting in London, 3 months later, Dr B had been unable to make it due to a Masonic Lodge meeting but joined the group at our London hotel for a nightcap at around 10.30 pm. I went to bed at around 11, but on checking out the following morning, I discovered 2 bottles of Bollinger Reserve added to my room bill, amounting to £450. I was fairly certain that I had only had beers. I paid up and emailed Dr B. The reply came back, "Oops, Champagne Charley strikes again!"

Despite our concerns we decided to take part in the Nitrate cream study. Our third patient, Mr Richard Head, was attending for his first visit on a day when the CEO of the company was onsite, dealing with some administrative issues. Richard, or Dick as he preferred, was very chatty, as I applied the first dose of the messy cream to his penis. We were just getting ready for the blood test and ECG, when he sat up, slumped forward, and crashed to the floor. It was time to implement all my CPR training. His airway was clear. I put him in the recovery position, ascertained that he was still breathing, and had a weak pulse. I suddenly thought that he would still be absorbing the drug, so pulled down his trousers and his pants and wiped all the surplus drug from his penis. It did cross my mind how the CCTV footage of the incident might look to the General Medical Council (GMC) in the event of formal investigation. Over the next 10 minutes, he recovered. We decided, of course that he should withdraw from the study and that we now needed to complete a serious adverse event form. I informed him that the CEO of the company was in the office and asked whether he would like to give him some feedback. "I certainly would", replied Dick, "Where is he?" I went into the office, only to learn that the CEO, having been told what was going on, had decided that he had a pressing appointment, compelling him to leave at short notice via the back door. Other investigators had similar experiences and multiple sites withdrew. Rather than accepting that this drug has no future for ED, the company continued to conduct trials of this product.

Around 2002, there was at last interest in treating post-menopausal women with low sexual desire. The difficulty in female trials was the lack of objective measurement, as erections and ejaculation are relatively simple to assess. Female symptoms could be more readily linked with depression, relationship problems, body image issues, menopausal symptoms, or indeed ED or PE in the partner. It was essential to screen women carefully, to exclude these other issues as much as possible. Investigators all required special training in the use of newly developed questionnaires specially for these studies. The first trial involved a low dose testosterone or placebo patch for post-menopausal women. The results were promising, and the patches were licensed in

2006, but for a narrow indication of women with a surgically induced premature menopause. By 2010, it was evident that this indication was too narrow for commercial success, and the patches were withdrawn.

The next important study was Flibanserin, a centrally acting drug developed to treat women before the menopause with acquired low sexual desire, meaning that the problem had not always been present. The media hailed this as "Pink Viagra" but, of course it was nothing remotely like a pink version of the blue pill. We were one of only 3 UK centres to conduct this trial meaning that, essentially, I am one of 3 UK doctors to have clinical experience with this drug. From our point of view the results seemed encouraging. We remember one woman who had never had a significant relationship but was able to meet a partner and get married as a result of the drug. They were absolutely delighted and thanked us profusely at the end of the trial, even inviting us to the wedding. Sadly, the trial ended, and the company were unable to provide further drug on "compassionate" grounds. We later heard that her problems returned, and she had split with her partner. This centrally acting drug to increase a woman's desire for sex encountered strong resistance from the feminist lobby in the US but was controversially licensed there in 2015. The drug has been moderately successful, as it seems to be effective in a selected group of women. There are no signs of a UK licence.

Another interesting Female project involved the use of a tiny vacuum device, called "Eros", which is placed over the clitoris (assuming the partner can find this elusive organ), and inflated by a pump. This increases blood flow and enhances arousal and orgasm. Eros remains a niche product that has never really become popular. A similar outcome was seen with "clitoral stimulator" that fitted over the finger to facilitate clitoral orgasm. Both these products are available on the internet. At the various specialist meetings, a prominent Scottish psychiatrist put forward the view that clitoral orgasm was a sign of an "immature sexual response" in contrast to vaginal orgasm. Rarely have I seen a subject cause such passion in a medical audience. Cultural circumcision is perhaps the only topic that came close.

Based on my clinical experiences with daily tadalafil in women, I approached the manufacturers, Lilly, recommending studies in women with "arousal "disorder. The problem with early studies of Viagra in women was that lack of desire is the main problem in women and that, without desire for sex, the motivation to take a tablet before sex is simply not there. Without appropriate HRT or testosterone therapy to restore desire, treatment was likely to fail. Unfortunately, around the time of the Viagra studies, the adverse publicity around HRT caused the companies to withdraw from this area of research. An additional problem was that post-menopausal women were likely to have a partner with ED, further complicating the issue. The only solution was to take tadalafil daily, enabling the woman to have sex spontaneously when the moment was right. Unfortunately, the timing was wrong for the company as they were already seeking other licensed indications for the drug and they reasonably argued that, by the time all the research was completed, their patient would have run out and there would be no profit. I still remain hopeful that future research will happen, as, based on my clinical experience, daily tadalafil is a very effective and safe drug for women with low sexual arousal. As you will see in the final chapter "serious stuff" there are other potential health benefits for women, including improvement in urinary symptoms.

I was at Waterford airport on May bank holiday Saturday, returning from an exhausting golf tournament in Ireland, when my phone went. Dr Bollinger's blood pressure was causing problems and he was advised to pull out of 2 presentations on Flibanserin at the American College of Obstetricians and Gynaecologists (ACOG) in New Orleans, commencing the following day. Dr B felt that I was the only person who could possibly stand at a day's notice. I had to say yes or no immediately as I would only have a few hours between flights. Realising that I still owed Dr B big time for presenting him as the media anal sex expert – the answer was yes. On arrival home, Sally was not amused that I was straight back to the airport again, but a glimpse at the contract and fee was greeted with the words "You must go". It was a great trip and most agreed that I was an adequate stand in for the great man.

In 2002, clinical trials for testosterone therapy in men were taking place, as new products were now available. Those most affected by low testosterone, termed hypogonadism, were men with type 2 diabetes, obesity, or those taking regular pain killers. The first study involved either active or placebo gel and yielded positive results. Based on this clear benefit, in 2006, I set up my own study of long acting testosterone Injection or placebo in 200 men with type 2 diabetes. This study was a career defining moment for me and there is much more about this in the chapter intitled "serious stuff". Through my excellent links with local general practices, we screened over 1000 patients to identify men for the study and have now continued to follow-up these men for 10 years. I negotiated the budget, devised the protocol, co-ordinated the centres and worked with a specialist statistician who managed the data and all statistical aspects of the study. We gave the study the acronym BLAST (Birmingham, Lichfield, Atherstone, Sutton Coldfield and Tamworth). After 5 years we found that 13.3% of those with normal testosterone had died, 20% of those with low testosterone UNTREATED but only 3.6% of those on treatment. Best results were seen in men over 70, perhaps the least likely men to receive a prescription from their GP. We also found that taking a tablet for ED also significantly lowered the risk of dying. There are 2 large studies expected in the next 3 years that will address these issues, but remember you heard it here first.

To date the BLAST project has yielded 14 papers and counting. It remains today the largest and longest placebo-controlled study of testosterone injection therapy in men with diabetes. Without doubt, treating men with low testosterone has been the most rewarding aspect of my medical practice, but more about that in the final chapter.

Over the last 25 years in sexual medicine, I have made many friends and contacts all over the world. There are many places around the world where I know that I could turn up and be treated like a long-lost friend, and they all know that the reverse is true. The unifying link is a sense of humour. If you cannot laugh about sex, then you cannot laugh about anything. This is reflected in much of the published research.

The most famous publication was the "Sex in the MRI scanner - 1991" from Sabellis et al in the Netherlands. This remains the most downloaded BMJ paper of all time. The author was also one of the 12 subjects who had sex within the scanner in the rear entry position. I had seen further papers presented by a French team at a later ESSM who decided to repeat the work, and why wouldn't one? My take home message had been the intense self-control required to keep absolutely still for 10 minutes after full penetration. Although dismissed by the editor as "hardly as important as the moon landing", we learned that the penis developed a boomerang shape with a third of the erect length being in the penile root. The vagina lengthened during sex and the uterus enlarged and rode up minimally. Other female subjects allowed images to be taken at various stages of masturbation adding much to what we previously knew about female orgasm.

Many studies have looked at the important issue of sex and athletic performance. An Italian study in 2008 suggested that football strikers were more likely to score after sex the night before. This reminded me of one of my boyhood heroes, the hugely talented 70s Leicester, Liverpool and England striker, Frank Worthington. In his autobiography "One hump or two", he reported regularly having sex at half time during first division matches. In contrast, world cup managers traditional banned sex before matches. Sven Goran Eriksen, famous for his own sexual exploits, encouraged WAGs at the 2006 world cup and England flopped. In 2010, Fabio Capello banned sex during the tournament and England flopped again. The reality is that sex consumes around 50 calories, the equivalent of climbing 2 flights of stairs, totally insignificant for a trained athlete. Boxing and Rugby coaches were worried that ejaculation might deplete testosterone and reduce aggression, whereas the evidence is that prolonged abstinence, certainly of longer than 3 months, significantly reduces testosterone and hence aggression.

In 2014, I was invited to take part in a fascinating project, the "Big Check Campaign", involving a potentially life-changing question, "Can you see your manhood?" This involved over 1000 men who attended for health checks and had their waste measurement check along with a question as to whether they could see their penis when they were standing naked and looking down. In the West Midlands, 43.33% of men between 45 and 70 could not see their penis, compared with 22.89% in the South-East. Being unable to see your penis as associated with a 5-fold risk of type-2 diabetes and 3-fold risk of colon cancer. As a result of this landmark study, my colleague, Professor Mike Kirby patented the" peniscope ", a modified periscope, to facilitate regular penis inspection in the West Midlands.

In 2014, I set out to see whether the Italian footballer study would be valid for older men playing golf. As mentioned earlier, a good acronym is important for any study, so I came up with the Sexual Habits of Ageing Golfers or SHAG study. The beauty of this study was that, whereas there are relatively few goals in Italian football, ageing golfers frequently take over 100 strokes per round. Conveniently, all shots are recorded on the golf club website as a statistical record of performance. I was advised by my statistician to start with a small pilot study to test the methodology. I gave 20 randomly selected golfers a record card to complete, recording the timing of sexual activity over a 3-month period and then downloaded their scores from that period. We found that there was a weak positive correlation between sex the night before a round with a mean 0.2 stroke improvement. Unfortunately, the frequency of sex in the ageing golfers was only 1-2 times per month. This allowed me to make 3 important conclusions:

Ageing UK golfers have significantly less sex than Italian footballers. Ageing UK golfers should probably have more sex. More studies were required.

I decided to apply for a 5S research grant (The Scandinavian Society for the Study of Sexual Statistics) and my pilot SHAG study was accepted for a poster presentation at the 5S conference in Sweden is 2015. On the plane to Stockholm, I found myself sitting next to a blonde Swedish Researcher, who spoke with great enthusiasm about her oral presentation on "Penile length and Girth – the 20-nation study". She had received an earlier society grant and had spent 3 years visiting 20 countries and measuring penile dimensions of 100 random males of matched age from each country. With great excitement, she told me that the results were to be revealed for the first time at the meeting but if I swore to keep her secret, she would reveal all. As we were getting on so well, I promised. She revealed that the longest penis at mean length 5.5 inches was the Native American Indian but the greatest girth at 4.02 inches were Italians, who, according to secondary end point, were also the best lovers. This should come as a surprise to nobody. Anxious to impress, I responded "Absolutely fascinating, I can hardly wait for the presentation, by the way, I haven't introduced myself, the name is Tonto Corleone". On this occasion, my grant application was unsuccessful.

Research from North Carolina State University hit the CNN headlines, a few years ago with the finding that women who practiced regular fellatio with swallowing significantly reduced their chances of breast cancer. I presented the findings at a couple of meetings over the next month. The research, conducted by Professor Kramer and his team followed two groups, 6,246 women ages 25 to 45 who had performed fellatio and swallowed on a regular basis over the past five to ten years, and 9,728 women who had not or did not swallow. The group of women who had performed and swallowed had a breast cancer rate of 1.9% and the group who had not had a breast cancer rate of 10.4%. The CNN website had a million hits in 2 days. It seemed that we had the definitive study showing the benefits of a particular type of regular sexual activity. A change in sexual habits was also endorsed by a New England Journal of Medicine paper in 2007, reporting that 58% of Americans aged 57-75 regularly practiced oral sex and even 31% of couples 75-85. This not only normalised the practice, but a man could now say that he was prioritising the health of his partner by “permitting” her to have fellatio. It was an Australian reporter who spotted that the lead researcher, Helena Shifteer stated "Since the emergence of the research, I try to fellate at least once every other night to reduce my chances." The CNN release went: Dr. Len Lictepeen, deputy chief medical officer for the American Cancer Society (very suspect now), said women should not overlook or "play down" these findings. "This will hopefully change women's practice and patterns, resulting in a severe drop in the future number of cases of breast cancer," Lictepeen said. "There's definitely fertile ground for more research. Many have stepped forward to volunteer for related research now in the planning stages," he said. Almost every woman is, at some point, going to perform the act of fellatio, but it is the frequency at which this event occurs that makes the difference. The key seems to be the protein and enzyme count in the semen, but researchers are again waiting for more test data.

Back in the real world of proper science, there is a growing evidence that supports some of these fantasies. For a start: "Oral sex makes pregnancies safer." It is true, research by Professor Gus Dekker, a maternal-foetal medicine specialist at the University of Adelaide, shows. Dekker compared 41 pregnant women with pre-eclampsia - a condition where the mother's blood pressure soars during pregnancy - to 44 without. He found 82% of those without the condition practised fellatio compared with 44% of those with it. The explanation? Semen contains a growth factor which helps persuade a mother's immune system to accept sperm. Regular exposure before pregnancy helps her immune system get used to her partner's sperm.

Stronger link between sex and cancer has been found in recent work by Professor Graham Giles and his Melbourne team, who found that men can reduce their risk of prostate cancer through regular ejaculation. Comparing the sexual habits of a group of 1000 men who had developed prostate cancer with 1250 who had not, they found men who ejaculated more than five times a week were a third less likely to develop prostate cancer later in life. Regular ejaculation may prevent carcinogens accumulating in the prostate gland, with no increased risk of blindness, suggest the researchers.

One of my favourite papers was published in the British Journal of Urology in 2019. This dealt with the delicate subject of Post Micturition Dribble (PMD), that embarrassing problem of an untimely leak just after you think that you have put the old chap away. It was a study of 102 Korean gentlemen who took either tadalafil or placebo daily. This research was not very heavy on technology. They placed a double folded paper towel down their trousers and walked around for one minute.

The towel was then removed and examined by an "expert". The leaked volume was 2ml on placebo and 1ml with tadalafil. This showing significant improvement with tadalafil in an underrated problem, for which no other drug had been effective. I wondered if this was a "spoof" when I saw that the author was Lee Ki Kok, but it was completely authentic.

Recent research has been devoted to finding "a cure" for ED. I worked with a cardiologist colleague in Cardiff who was investigating the arteries supplying blood to the penis. He was attempting to reverse the blockages by inserting stents, in the same way that we treat coronary artery disease. After anecdotal success, results were not sustained and funding for this research has been withdrawn.

A number of papers from Israel and Turkey have reported the benefit of shock waves applied to the penis with multiple treatments over several weeks. Impressed with the results, I purchased a machine and began recording my results. It soon became evident that I could not offer treatment in the NHS as it was not NICE endorsed. Even in the private hospital, rules prevented consultants from bringing in their own equipment because of legal liability. The only solution was to rent rooms in a GP surgery. Because of the price of the equipment and the need for 10-12 treatments involving at least 45 minutes of specialist time, the cost to the patient was prohibitive. The problem with new treatments, is that initially we treat the "desperate" patients who have failed with everything else. It is hardly surprising that the results are often disappointing. My personal opinion is that shock wave therapy will only be beneficial for milder patients, where tablets will always be a cheaper and more logical alternative. It may also be helpful in cases where tablets are almost effective, converting men to full responders. For that reason, most trials now combine shock wave therapy with daily tadalafil.

In the last 12 months, stem cell therapy has emerged as a practical treatment for ED. This usually involves the injection of stem cells extracted from the patient's own fat samples removed from the abdominal fat through liposuction. These stem cells have the power to promote tissue healing and recovery if injected elsewhere, in this case into the penis. Currently men are paying tens of thousands of pounds to visit clinics in the Bahamas or even Russia or India. My first patient underwent treatment in India in 2019. This involved the use of cells from the placenta of a new-born baby, potentially the best stem cells of all. There is no way this would achieve ethics approval in the UK. Six months on there was no improvement at all despite spending nearly £20,000. Of course, such anecdotal cases prove nothing, but it is difficult to remain enthusiastic when the next patient presents. It is a major problem when patients turn up having read about some sensational new treatment online claiming miracle cures. They fail to realise that sites have usually been paid to promote these products under the guise of new discoveries. Our role as physicians is to protect the vulnerable public from such predators.

The work never stops. Across the world male scientists beaver away trying to prove the benefits of sex. The search for cures for sexual problems in men and women continues. It has been fascinating to be part of that journey for over 25 years.

I now realised that this was what I wanted to do.

CHAPTER 9.
The Serious Stuff

"In my opinion, people who continually make sweeping stereotypical generalisations are all the same"
— Geoff Hackett 2019.

Thirty years specialising in sexual medicine and men's health has taught me many lessons. I will attempt to pass many of these on to the reader in this chapter. A 2018 government research study on happiness in the US found that relationships were rated as most important, followed by health. I would hope, that after reading the earlier chapters, the reader will agree that solving sexual problems ticks both these boxes. Preventing relationship breakdown has huge social and financial impact for society.

In many ways, men are their own worst enemies. They take more risks. They drink too much, smoke too much, experiment with drugs, drive too fast, fight too much, and engage in dangerous activities. In addition, they rarely see doctors between the ages the ages of 12 and 40, except for accidents and injuries, usually associate with risk taking and alcohol. Women consult health care professions 3 times more often than men up to the age of 60, after which events catch up with men and they consult just as often.

Men die on average 4 years earlier than women and this "gender gap" is greater in certain parts of the country such as the North East. In fact, life expectancy for men can be 6-7 years less in men in the most deprived versus the most affluent areas. Men's have higher rates of death from cardiovascular disease such as heart attack and stroke. Men also have higher rates of type 2 diabetes and increased associated mortality. They also have higher mortality from all types of cancer, excluding the "sex specific" ones such as breast, uterus, and ovary. This increased mortality is largely related to late diagnosis. An excellent example is malignant melanoma of the skin. Women get more melanoma, but men die much more frequently, because they present later.

The real question is "What can we as men do about this?". The first answer to that question is that we cannot rely on the health care system to sort this out for us. As GPs are essentially "self-employed contractors", they have responded to the demands of their clients. If three times as many women come to see the doctor, then the service they provide has developed to address those needs. This is essentially the same response that any business would take to assess their client base in order to retain and attract new clients. If the general practice demand is for consultations related to contraception, maternity, mother and baby, breast screening, HRT, well women, then the health care appointments and personnel have been tailored to meet these demands. If the service is not met, patients will go elsewhere. This certainly means that the reading matter in the surgery is more likely to be "Hello" or "OK" rather than "Top Gear" or "Golf Monthly".

Very commonly a woman will be greeted at reception with the words "Well, Mrs Brown, you'll be wanting an appointment for one of our lady doctors". Often the patient is not asked, it is the assumption of the virtually 100% female reception staff that this will be the case. The result of the increase in demand for female consultations led some years ago to a positive discrimination towards medical school places. A General Medical Council report in 2015 showed that 59% of GPs under 50 were female versus 37% over 50. The corresponding figures for hospital specialists was 38% and 25%.

The primary care gender issue is worsened by the way GPs are remunerated. Whereas a percentage of GP incomes is from "capitation fees", essentially the numbers on their list, a substantial element of income is from "item for service payments". In the case of female patients, income will clock up with contraception, maternity, breast and cervical screening, and well-woman and menopause visits in some cases. There are no male specific payments. Although prostate screening has been introduced in many countries, the UK stance has always been that such a programme would not be cost effective. We therefore have a situation, whereby any female registering with a GP is a much better financial deal for the practice. Likewise, a female GP might also represent better value. It would, of course, be illegal for any practice to accept female patients in preference or for any practice to advertise for a specific gender of a doctor. The reality was that, if I was to hold a clinic in one room seeing men with erection problems whereas a lady partner for in the next room running a contraceptive clinic, I would bring zero income to the practice, whereas she would bring in several hundred pounds. I would also receive a visit from the community pharmacist for being a prescribing "outlier", in terms of ED medication, which would come with financial penalties. If I were to attempt to justify my prescribing because I was offering a better service, this would be perceived as arrogant and critical of other practitioners.

In 2013, it appeared that NICE had finally got the message when they introduced a payment policy for GPs in return for asking men with diabetes about their erections once a year. As evidence, they cut and pasted the submission that we had provided 7 years earlier. At that time, NICE invited the Tsar, Professor Mike Kirby and Dr David Edwards, a GP from Chipping Norton to a meeting in Birmingham to discuss this subject. We invited Dr Graham Jackson to join us. We then received a message from NICE to say that he must not attend, because "he knows too much"! From that day on Graham Jackson lived with that title. In fact, at ISSM in Beijing in 2016, after his death, I was invited to do a memorial lecture in his honour entitled, "Dr Graham Jackson, the man who knew too much". It seemed no accident that this payment to GPs coincided with the availability of cheap generic sildenafil. Immediately GPs hit the 80% target and collected the cash. Twelve months later the payments were withdrawn on the basis of "simplification". A year on we were back to square one with only 10% of men being asked. If ever there was an example of what was needed to improve outcomes in men's heath, this was it.

In 2015, I conducted an audit of GP practice websites involving 262 GPs (142 female and 120 male). Whereas 68% of female doctors expressed an interest in women's health, only 1% of male doctors expressed an interest in men's health, and he was working for me as a clinical assistant and has since retired. In 2018, the chance of a patient finding a GP who has a declared interest in men's health would be negligible. Having been involved in training and motivation of GPs for over 25 years, we still have only a handful of GPs with an interest in men's health scattered around the country. Most of these are getting older with little sign of younger ones coming through to fill the gap. In contrast, there are a significant number of private menopause clinics, employing GPs with passionate interest in women's health.

There are 14 Women's hospitals in the UK and no Men's hospitals. When I am at a loose end, I often drive to the reception of Birmingham Women's hospital and ask for the Men's hospital just to see the reaction. In other European Countries and the US, Men's hospitals do exist, often termed Andrology Departments but few men or women in the UK would know what this term means. As mentioned in earlier chapters, medical students receive extensive training in women's health and virtually nothing than addresses the needs of men. The Royal College of GPs has a spokesperson on women's health but not one for men. I ring the RCGP from time to time asking for this non-existent person and often encounter the response, "Why would we possibly need a men's health spokesman?". The answer is, is of course, that men have the greatest need. If research had identified an ethnic or religious group who were suffering from health inequalities, there would be an immediate government initiate to address this. Finally, there is even a government minister for women, and not one for men. All these issues led me to give talks and write articles entitled "Short, Brutal and Nasty – it's a Man's life".

Men are not going to change their behaviour overnight, and women have the right to expect the highest standards of healthcare to address their needs. Their preference to have this delivered by physicians of their choice must be appreciated. The physicians providing these important services also deserve to be paid appropriately for the work being done. Women might also argue that we should not be funding drugs for men's sexual satisfaction from precious NHS resources when no such therapies exist for women. It is therefore totally understandable that the NHS pharmacists have targeted these drugs for potential cost savings. The reality is that, in 2020, an entire 12 months treatment with sildenafil treatment costs the same as *a single tablet of Viagra in 1998,* and a prescription charge costs roughly ten times more than the real cost of a month's supply of drug. Four years after the licence of Viagra, two further drugs, tadalafil (Cialis) and vardenafil (Levitra) were also licensed and these are now also available in cheaper generic form. The recent crisis in the NHS due to Covid19, with cancellation of routine services, is likely to lead to an appraisal as to what the public can expect from the NHS in future. It is unlikely that such discussions will target morning erections and "mojo preservations" as top priorities for the future.

If we accept that there are inequalities in health care that the NHS are failing to address, we need to be practical as to what can be done to address these issues. The only solution is for men is to take control of their own health and this concept will form the basis of the rest of the chapter.

Hardly a day goes by without an article pointing out that we are facing an epidemic of obesity and type 2 diabetes and the UK is third only to the US and Mexico in this respect. Mediterranean countries figure much better in this respect. In the UK, the population of men from south east Asia, and particularly the Indian sub-continent, are at especially increased risk. The fundamental process at play is "Insulin resistance", meaning that these tissues are less sensitive to the effects of insulin and the body produces more insulin to try to counter this resistance. The higher levels of insulin are associated with increased "Inflammation" and the production of "Inflammatory proteins" that damage our arteries through a process called "oxidative stress". Whenever you read about vitamins and supplements, you will see that the main claim for benefit will usually be that as "anti-oxidants", they reduce this oxidative stress.

The clear advice would be to switch to a Mediterranean type diet rather than a US high carbohydrate type. The Mediterranean diet is essentially based on whole grains, fish, olive oil and nuts, fresh vegetables and fruit with red meat confined to once per week. There is considerable evidence to support the long-term health benefits including weight reduction and reduced insulin resistance. Rather depressingly, a 2020 study in the British Medical Journal reviewed 15 types of diet across a host of clinical trials and confirmed that they are all equally successful over a 6-month period but lose their effect by 12 months. These findings suggest that fundamental changes to the dietary patterns of a lifetime are very difficult to maintain. The counter argument, of course, is that unless you do lose weight in the first place, you are unlikely to be in the 10% who maintain that weight loss. In recent years, the basis of the NHS approach has been to turn the responsibility back onto the patient to modify their own health and reduce the burden on the NHS.

The benefits of exercise on insulin resistance are clear. A 45-minute episodes of moderate aerobic exercise will improve insulin resistance for 16 hours. The important point is that the move from no exercise to a moderate level show the greatest benefit. Walking, jogging, and cycling are sufficient forms of exercise and there is little additional benefit in pushing exercise levels to excess.

We should, of course, look to reduce unnecessary stress in our lives and focus on our most important relationships, especially with our partner. We should discuss openly what is important to us in the relationship and listen to their wishes. We should try to negotiate a common ground and do not let old feuds continue. We should concentrate on what brought us together. It might have been sexual attraction, so we need to work on returning to sex and intimacy the way it was, as much as possible. Forgive, forget, and move on. Whilst on clichés, Life is not a rehearsal, so do not put these things off. Get them sorted now and start enjoying life again.

I now move on to some more specific advice. A man's erections, especially the spontaneous ones in the morning are the best predictor of a man's heart health. This has been shown many times and every study has come to the same conclusions. Men should rejoice over every firm morning erection. If you can hang a towel over it, then sing hallelujah! As a leading American Cardiologist said in the 80s, "If you can't get an erection, your heart is heading in the wrong direction". A question about your erection should be part of every health check at your GP surgery. It is more important than asking about smoking. If the doctor or nurse forgets, remind them. Only by constantly reminding them, will they get the message. Likewise, anyone paying a fortune for a private health medical should point out that failure to ask about erections means that the medical is not fit for purpose. Studies show that the average interval between losing erections and a cardiac event is 3-5 years, so a man cannot wait for a doctor to get around to asking.

The aspiration of every doctor is to have a disease, clinical sign, or test named after them. I would like to present my major contribution to medical science, *Hackett's 2 cough test.* Men with high blood pressure in the UK are usually treated with a drug called ramipril, which belongs to a class called Angiotensin Converting Enzyme (ACE) inhibitors. These have a slightly adverse effect on erections and a bothersome side effect of an irritating cough in 15-20% of patients. An alternative and slightly superior drug would be valsartan or losartan, a group called Angiotensin Receptor Blockers (ARBs), which improve erections. Whenever I asked GPs to switch the medication to improve a man's erection, they completely ignored my suggestion. I then decided to tell the patient to give a little cough at the start of the consultation. The GP would usually stop for a few seconds, but with a second cough, they would ask the patient when this cough started. An answer of "Shortly after starting those blood pressure tablets", would result in an immediate switch from ACE to ARB, with improved erections. Hackett's "two cough test" works every time. In mild cases of ED, this medication switch may be all that is required.

Forty per cent of men aged 40 and 50 per cent aged 50 suffer from erectile dysfunction (ED) and these men are at 46% increased risk of a heart attack and need investigation. Do not let a doctor tell you that this is "normal" (so is death) or "just due to stress". Do not accept advice to "chill out" or "man-up". In some cases, if a man has excellent morning erections but loses them during sex, then "performance anxiety" may be an issue but cases should never be dismissed as this without investigation. Excellent performance with one partner but not with another, termed situational ED, would also suggest performance anxiety. **All** men with ED need their blood pressure and heart checked plus bloods tests for **diabetes, cholesterol, and a morning testosterone level**, ideally with a test called SHBG (sex hormone binding globulin). SHBG is a compound that is produced by the liver. It tightly binds to testosterone rendering it inactive and therefore, reducing the amount of free “active” testosterone in the circulation. SHBG rises with age and is the main cause of the fall in free testosterone as we get older.

The Health Benefits of Sex

In earlier chapters, I described the benefits of sexual activity in reducing the risk of cardiac death by 50% in men having sex more than twice per week. This has been confirmed in at least 3 studies. A study from Sweden also showed benefits of regular sex but quality was more than quantity when it came to women. The Tampere study from Scandinavia showed that regular sex reduced the chances of developing ED and another study showed that men who were not having morning erections developed structural changes in the penis, which could become irreversible with time. These studies effectively demonstrate that the adage of "Use it or lose it" is 100% true. It is therefore important that we do not simply treat this evidence with a smutty giggle but embrace it proactively.

"You know, darling, since we've been having sex twice a day, I think I'm looking 10 years younger."

Loss of Erections is an important warning sign of Heart Disease.

The importance of ED as an early warning sign of heart disease cannot be overstated. The mechanism for this is explained by the "Arterial Size Hypothesis". The process by which the arteries function poorly is termed "Endothelial Dysfunction". Our arteries are lined with a thin layer of cells called the endothelium. If this thin layer, like clingfilm, covering all our arteries was peeled off, it would cover a tennis court. If this layer is damaged, then cholesterol is deposited on the damaged areas, leading to "plaque" which will narrow the arteries. " The arteries to the penis are 60% of the diameter of the coronary arteries and ED appears when there is around 50% narrowing. In contrast men can have 70% narrowing of a coronary artery without any symptoms. We regularly put our penis through this "stress test" every time we have sex, whereas we might rarely put our heart to such stress testing. If the appearance of ED comes 3-5 years before a heart attack, then the clock is running. Action needs to be taken promptly to diagnose and address all the factors that are narrowing the arteries. These include diabetes, high blood pressure and raised cholesterol. The important message is that if you have ED, these problems should be addressed much more pro-actively rather just token efforts to "exercise more and eat less fat". Many cardiologists believe that "a man with ED has heart disease until proven otherwise". Others would prescribe a statin to lower cholesterol in all men with persistent ED. We are clearly dealing with a chronic disease process here and it is vital to treat the disease process and not just a symptom.

The Importance of Prostate Disease

As men age, they develop more symptoms related to their prostate, that small gland, normally the size of a walnut (25ml), situated just below the bladder. Traditionally we thought that this was a simple matter of the prostate growing with age, but we now know that prostate symptoms, such as going to pee more often, poor stream, delay in peeing, dribbling and getting up more at night are closely related to ED, diabetes, high blood pressure and raised cholesterol. Essentially the prostate is also a victim of insulin resistance, oxidative stress, and poor blood supply. If left untreated, men will often need surgery to address these symptoms in later life. I need to emphasise that this is Benign Prostate Enlargement and not Prostate Cancer, although regular sex and more frequent ejaculation has also been shown to reduce the risk of prostate cancer. Daily tadalafil has been licensed to treat enlarged prostate for several years and has been advocated as first line treatment across Europe for men with both ED and enlarged prostate. Unfortunately, NICE, in the UK have never produced guidelines on ED and declined to consider tadalafil when they produced prostate guidelines, due to a dispute with the manufacturer over the agenda, which failed to consider possible benefits of treating ED in the same patient. Tadalafil 5mg daily, apart from improving symptoms, increases blood supply to the prostate and reduces inflammation. This mechanism is highly likely to significantly improve the overall health of the prostate, but the long-term clinical trials that we need will take several years. Men in their 50s and 60s now do not have the time to wait for these perfect studies. Most urologists realised these benefits of daily tadalafil and have been taking it for years, in my case 12. The benefits were brought home to me when I popped into the loo just off the patient waiting room one day. As I emerged, two ladies were sitting just outside and one said “Oh, it’s you doctor, we through a horse was loose in the building”. As physicians, we need to give best advice based on our current knowledge and experience.

The role of ED drugs

In 1998, Viagra, the first of a group of drugs called Phosphodiesterase Type 5 Inhibitors (PDE5-Is) were licensed. We all got use to the concept of taking a “blue pill” an hour before sex and being told they “might be dangerous”. PDE5-Is work by increasing the level of a chemical called Nitric Oxide (NO) in the blood vessels, and other tissues. NO opens the blood vessels and increases blood flow. The discovery that this increase in blood flow in the penis could produce an erection was a chance finding in trials where the drug was being used to treat heart disease. The decision of the manufacturers to focus on ED was a commercial one but it should come as no surprise that these drugs are also very good at what they were developed for – heart disease. This raises 2 important issues. Firstly, a beneficial drug should not be restricted to once per week, as the function of the penis needs to be improved 7 days per week, not just for 1 hour on a Saturday night. Secondly, if men with ED have undiagnosed heart disease, then surely taking a drug that is good for the heart would be sensible.

Let us deal with the idea that these drugs might be dangerous. In the early stages, men with advanced heart disease, unable to walk more than a few yards without chest pain, decided to "roll back the years" with long nights of passion. As sex involves physical effort, equivalent to walking a mile in 20 minutes or climbing 2 flights of stairs, clearly the hearts of these men were not capable of this level of effort. They were also unlikely to heed the warning signs especially after a large meal and bottle of wine. The problem with Viagra (sildenafil) is that it is short acting and would need to be given 2-3 times per day, whereas the second drug in this group, tadalafil lasts more than 4 times longer, so is suitable for daily dosing. ED, as explained earlier is part of a chronic disease process namely endothelial dysfunction. Taking a tablet before sex treats a *symptom*, whereas taking a daily medication treats the disease process (endothelial dysfunction). When a man goes online, or to the pharmacy for Viagra Connect, he is not treating the disease process, which will continue to develop. In 2-3 years, the narrowing will have progressed, and the Viagra will stop working. By this stage, other arteries will also have narrowed, and the heart attack may be quick to follow. Daily medication treats the disease process, as well as the symptoms. Recent studies show that daily therapy with PDE5-Is significantly reduce the risks of a heart attack.

The problem was that having been licensed nearly 4 years later than Viagra, there was a long period where tadalafil was much more expensive, such that the NHS would have been in considerable financial difficulties had these theories been allowed to develop. For example, between 2014 and 2018, generic sildenafil was 17p per tablet and branded Cialis was £55 per month. The NHS response was to only endorse

Sildenafil and ban the use of Cialis, creating the impression that there might be some "concerns" about the drug. In late 2017, tadalafil became generic and the NHS price for the daily dose fell to £5-6, or around £9 per month on private prescription. The NHS continues to endorse only sildenafil and at 4 tablets per month for 80p rather than 28 tablets of tadalafil at £5-6. This has created a very difficult problems for specialists. Patients referred to hospitals will have been tried and failed of the regime of 4 Sildenafil per month, the only one provided at NHS cost. All other medications now have to be funded privately. Daily Tadalafil works in half of these patients but men cannot understand why they must pay privately, even if they are 75 and on benefits.

I now dread the question "What would be the best treatment for me to take, doctor?" Should I give the honest answer based on the latest information from international conferences and publications, or should I state the official NHS policy, even if I know it to be financially based and 5 years out of date. Most doctors working in the NHS will, without hesitation, recite verbatim the official NHS position with no mention of any alternative approach. The General Medical Council, however, informs us that we must be open and honest with patients at all time. The mission statement of my hospital trust was CARING, ACCOUNTABLE, SUPPORTIVE and <u>HONEST</u>. Many of you will notice that this acronym spells CASH.

Beyond a shadow of a doubt, that "best" treatment is tadalafil 5mg daily, but I will now be contradicting their GP and his NHS advisers, who continue to be unaware of the progressive research on this subject as, after all, "It isn't a matter of life and death, is it?". I would suggest that a heart attack in 3-5 years is actually a matter of life and death.

Benefits beyond ED

Having convinced you that treating your penis with a daily tablet allows for the return of morning erections and the ability to have sex spontaneously when both of you are in the mood, the way it used to be, I would like to expand the argument. Several studies show that partners dislike orchestrated sex once per week, especially in new relationships when a man might be too embarrassed to mention that he takes medication.

From now on I will refer to tadalafil 5mg as it is the only licensed treatment for daily use. I hope the reader will stop using Viagra as the generic name for these drugs in the way we talk of buying a Hoover, even though we have bought Dysons for the last 10 years.

If tadalafil was developed to treat Heart Disease, it should surprise none of us that it is licensed to treat certain cardiac diseases, especially Pulmonary Hypertension, a very serious condition where the effect of the drug is to relax the walls of arteries and allow increased blood flow thereby lowering the raised pressure in the arteries in the lungs. Men taking daily tadalafil have been consistently shown to increase their exercise time on a treadmill by 10-20%, due to the dilating effect on coronary arteries.

Three recent studies have shown very consistent cardiac benefits. A 2016 UK study in nearly 6000 men with type 2 diabetes showed a 31% reduction in deaths over a 7.5-year period, in men who took a PDE5-I. There were similar reductions in all non-fatal events. A 2017 Study from Sweden looked at 43,145 men after previous heart attacks and found a 38% reduction in mortality in men over just 3.3 years taking a

PDE5-I. They also found that the effect was dose related and that men having a heart attack were 40% more likely to survive the heart attack if taking a PDE5-I. My own BLAST study involving nearly 1000 men with diabetes, showed a 40% reduction in mortality in men taking PDE5-Is.

Blood flow to the lower limbs correspondingly improves, an important finding for men with diabetes or smokers, who run into trouble with narrowing to blood vessels to extremities. PDE5-Is are effective in Raynaud's disease and patients with cold hands and feet in winter. Tadalafil increases blood flow to the kidneys and large muscles, where much of the problems of glucose metabolism and insulin resistance are seen. Trials show consistently that insulin resistance improves, interestingly more so in women, and that the inflammatory tests associated with heart disease also improve.

Recent studies have shown that tadalafil increases blood flow to the brain, improving tests of cognitive function, suggestive a possible preventive role for age related dementia.

A study from Sweden, evaluated 4600 men at risk for colon cancer being followed up with colonoscopy. Men taking a PDE5-I had a 40% decreased rate of colon cancer. There are possible complicating issues with these studies, as, in many countries, men need to pay privately for ED drugs, meaning that potentially they might be of higher socio-economic status, potentially biasing the findings. Unfortunately, the perfect placebo-controlled studies required to answer these questions will never be done for cost, commercial and logistic reasons.

What about Prevention of ED?

The vitamin and supplement market in the UK are worth £1bn per year up by 13.8% over the last 5 years. Most vitamins are taken for their ant-oxidant properties, aimed at reducing oxidative stress and reducing inflammation. The evidence for most of these effects suggest mild or tenuous benefit, whereas the findings in relation to tadalafil have been published in multiple placebo-controlled studies in peer review medical journals. This raises the question as to whether we should spend our hard-earned money on compounds that "might" work, or a drug established to work based on evidence-based research. When we are ill, we choose to consult specialists using tried and tested therapies, rather than visiting a herbalist, so why should it be different if we are trying to prevent serious disease? If we know that we have a 40% chance of ED by age 40 and 50% by age 50, isn't a problem that common worth preventing? It might be a good idea to save your first marriage rather than waiting for your second. Likewise, if we have a 30% chance of requiring surgery for enlarged prostate, is not the miserable prospect of waking several times at night worth preventing, as the benefits of daily tadalafil treatment for these conditions is beyond any dispute. The possibility of preserving renal function, improving mental function, and reducing dementia, reducing heart attack and cancer risk making a compelling argument for taking a small daily dose of a PDE5-I such as tadalafil. In terms of other supplements, high dose L-arginine (3G daily) and Carnitine (500mg) are amino-acid precursors that may have some additional benefit on ED, along with saw palmetto, ginseng and fo-ti (Chinese climbing knotweed). Commercial products using combinations of these drugs continue to be produced claiming "miracle" benefits for ED and the prostate. Unfortunately, the doses in commercial products are usually too low to produce any benefit. The effects are slight at best, yet there is little control over the sensational claims that can be made. In contrast, a licensed pharmaceutical product is subject to strict regulation and breach would attract potentially huge fines. Certainly, a man should take Vitamin D if he has a low level, especially Afro-Caribbean or South Asian men, and Folic acid 5mg daily in type 2 diabetes or men taking certain drugs for epilepsy.

In summary, I would advise that all men take daily tadalafil 5mg if they have type 2 diabetes, even if they do not have ED. I would advise all men to take it daily at the first sign of ED, rather than wait for spontaneous resolution, as the longer that ED is left untreated, the more difficult it will be to treat. I would also recommend all men over the age of 50 to consider regular dosing for all the clear multiple benefits. If we wait for this advice to become mainstream, it will be too late for many men who are over 50 now. It is highly unlikely that NHS funders would ever view the concept of ED prevention as a top priority. The reality is that, just as the NHS would not be expected to fund vitamin supplements, or indeed gym memberships, the burden of drugs to prevent ED will fall on the patient. As we already have Viagra over the counter, daily tadalafil is certain to follow. These drugs are extremely safe and eminently suitable for direct to public sale. This is the likely way that these issues will be resolved.

The importance of Testosterone (T)

Hypogonadism or testosterone deficiency is one of the most controversial issues in medicine and alone, the topic could fill a book three times this size. The condition is divided into PRIMARY, affecting 2% of the male population, where the problem lies in the testicles, which are failing to produce T, and SECONDARY, affecting 10%, where the problem lies at a higher level, usually in the pituitary gland. The pituitary gland can be affected by several chronic diseases and medications. What we do know is that having a low testosterone level is bad news. There is a 3 to 4-fold increase risk of type 2 diabetes and several studies have shown strong associations with early death. Many doctors decline to measure testosterone, feeling that it is better not to know, for fear of opening “Pandora’s box”. The most common reason for checking testosterone is ED, as ALL men should be checked, Low testosterone is a potentially treatable cause of ED, and a reason why conventional tablets might be less effective.

Do not accept that your testosterone level has been checked and is “Normal.” Always ask what the value actually is. So called normal values are in fact the “reference range” drawn to from the manufacturers who took 100 samples from healthy volunteers. They then classified the top 2.5% and the bottom 2.5% as abnormal and the other 95% as normal. These values have no relationship as to who might benefit from treatment. International Expert Guidelines Recommend that a level of above 12 nmol/l is accepted as normal. Tests should be done in the morning and preferably fasting. Healthy young men usually have levels between 18 and 30 nmol/l. As levels fall, more symptoms appear. Below 15, men might feel that they have less sexual desire, less enjoyment of life, less "get up and go". As levels fall below 12, tiredness, loss of strength, reduced morning erections, poor concentration, poor sleep, weight gain, diabetes and depression appear. Below 10 nmol/l, ED and sweating occur.

Over the last 20 years, I have diagnosed and successfully treated well over 1000 men with low testosterone. These men were often barely able to function in their normal lives. They were falling asleep at work, sometimes at the wheel of a car or van, and invariably at home in the evening. They were underachieving at work and in their marriages. For years, I have tried to persuade large companies, to screen middle aged and obese men in their occupational health services. The answer has always been that "we don't want to open a Pandora's box". In 2014, I wrote up a series of underperforming doctors with low testosterone, successfully treated and able to resume work and relationships successfully. If none of us would want to be treated by surgeon working at 70% of his capacity, why should this be acceptable in any occupation?

The reality is that whilst you might be concerned that you have lost interest in sex or lost your "mojo", this is unlikely to be a priority for the NHS, especially as treatment is relatively expensive. As Frank Dobson, Health Secretary in 1998 famously said in a provocative statement, "the NHS is not about helping middle-aged men to strut their stuff in discos".

Apart from the above symptoms, low testosterone is associated with increased obesity, with 3-4 times greater risk of type 2 diabetes, **earlier death from multiple causes associated with increased frailty**. They also have an increased risk of more aggressive prostate cancer. Several special groups are at increased risk of low testosterone, those with:

- **Obesity (especially men from South Asia)**
- **Type 2 diabetes (especially men from South Asia)**
- Long term painkillers, such as co-codamol, tramadol, or opiate abusers.
- Heart Failure, Heart Attack.
- HIV.
- Chronic Kidney Disease.
- Current or past users of anabolic steroids, especially for body-building purposes
- Men who have lost a testicle through cancer, trauma, or associated with radio- or chemotherapy.

A major international study of 1007 men with "pre-diabetes", the T4DM study has reported in June 2020. This study involved obese men with testosterone of less than 14 nmol/l randomised to intensive diet and exercise intervention PLUS either long acting testosterone injection of placebo injection, followed up for 2 years. The testosterone treated men had a 40% lower rate of progression to type 2 diabetes. Based on UK data, results from T4DM suggest that potentially over 1 million men might be prevented from progression to type 2 diabetes if their low testosterone was addressed.

The men in T4DM on testosterone also lost more fat, especially from the waist, gained muscle mass, and improved physical strength. These findings represent a major breakthrough in diabetes prevention. It is now vital that all obese or overweight men with or without ED insist on getting their testosterone level checked. Although men on diet and placebo had modest weight loss, their sexual function was actually worse after 2 years. The T4DM study should change future clinical practice in the UK.

The Impact of Covid-19 in 2020.

It is well published that 2/3 of Covid-19 deaths have been in men, usually over 70 and with the chronic diseases listed above. Suggested mechanisms were that men present later to doctors, take more risks, wash their hands less often and smoke more cigarettes. Surprisingly, although smoking rates are a little lower in women, they are more likely to get COPD (Chronic Obstructive Pulmonary Disease) and respiratory failure as their lungs are smaller and more vulnerable to the effects of both active and passive smoking.

Much has focused on the higher death rate in South Asian Men, but the reason for this is quite obvious. Men from Bangladesh, India and Pakistan have 3 times the rate of type 2 diabetes, due to genetic factors, combined with poor diet and lifestyle. These higher levels of diabetes and obesity lead to testosterone levels being 10-15% lower. In addition, smoking rates are 3 times higher than in white UK men. Forty-Four per cent of Bangladeshi men smoke, 26% of Indian and 23% of Pakistan men, although in stark contrast with UK white population, only around 1% of South Asian women smoke. Likewise, Afro-Caribbean men suffer from more severe and aggressive blood pressure, often unresponsive to conventional therapies. This results in higher rates of heart disease and stroke with shorter life expectancy. For genetic reasons have higher risks of Prostate Cancer and are monitored more closely for this. Likewise, certain jobs, such as taxi-drivers, and security guards have been associated with increased mortality, as it well established that such jobs are associated with higher rates of obesity and diabetes.

These health issues have been known for years, but the Covid-19 crisis has polarised views with some blaming social suppression of ethnic groups for the increased deaths. In reality, the healthcare system has been actively targeting these groups for years with variable success. Hopefully, the post-mortem after Covid-19 will see more positive interventions to improve outcomes for these higher risk populations.

At some stage, UK experts will realise that if all these men die more readily with these chronic conditions, such as type 2 diabetes when they have low testosterone, then surely, we would expect a serious predator (or mugger as Boris prefers) like Covid-19 to pick of these vulnerable patients with great efficiency. Studies from Germany and Italy have already shown that men with low testosterone levels on admission to hospital are significantly more likely to die. The lower the level of testosterone on admission, the greater the mortality rate. Studies from China show that the Covid-19 virus attacks the testosterone producing cells of the testis, causing further significant falls in levels and increased mortality. Studies from Italy have suggested that men with prostate cancer on anti-testosterone therapy had better outcome than those not on therapy. It appears that the mechanism of Covid-19 entering the cells of the body is enabled by testosterone, explaining why men fare less well than women. This had led to suggestions that drugs that lower testosterone might be helpful in the *acute stage of the illness*. In the long term these drugs are associated with side effects such as increased heart disease, diabetes, osteoporosis, depression, sexual dysfunction, and reduced quality of life. Limited trials in acute Covid-19 are under way. A couple of small studies suggesting bald men do less well with Covid-19 is likely to prove purely anecdotal as rates of baldness in different populations differ considerably, and sick Covid-19 patients in ITU units are likely to have "bad hair days".

Implications for the future

Multiple guidelines already recommended that men in high risk groups above should be checked and that low levels of testosterone should be treated. In the UK we have not been following this guidance. The message from this pandemic is clear. All men in the above groups should ensure that their testosterone level is checked. It the level is below 12 nmol/l, this needs to be treated, to improve symptoms, quality of life and to reduce vulnerability to future pandemics. The recent T4DM study from Australia suggested that benefits in preventing diabetes might even be seen with treating men at levels of 14 nmol/l.

In spite of this logical connection, there has been more interest in the UK as to why HRT might be protecting women. Whilst emergency measures and vaccine development are vitally important, during the pandemic, reducing the risks for vulnerable patients is equally important in the long term.

The bottom line is that men need to be aware of the problems of low testosterone themselves and not rely on doctors making the diagnosis for them. These issues are often considered as "lifestyle problems" and not part of general NHS care. Men need to accept that they need to be pro-active and seek investigation, diagnosis, and treatment in the private sector. There are many private laboratories who arrange home diagnostic testing.

Dealing with Myths

Testosterone is an emotional subject and most people have a view on the subject. The first myth to deal with is that testosterone therapy causes prostate cancer. In fact, evidence suggests the opposite, as older man get prostate cancer, and those with the lowest testosterone levels get more aggressive prostate cancer. Recently studies suggest that men who have been treated effectively for prostate cancer, have fewer recurrences if their low testosterone is corrected. Of course, many will want to wait for the perfect long -term trial, but it is unlikely that this study will ever be done.

The second myth is that testosterone therapy increases cardiac risk. Multiple trials have shown that restoring testosterone levels to normal reduces death due all causes including heart disease. The confusion arises from reports of increased cardiac events in the Anabolic Steroid community where doses several times higher than those required for replacement are commonly used in an unregulated fashion.

Replacing testosterone to normal levels is not usually associated with baldness or acne but can be associated with a slight reduction in testicular volume and infertility. These issues can usually be managed by subtle changes in therapy.

Possible benefits of testosterone therapy

After 40 years of medical practice, I continue to be surprised with the benefits of testosterone therapy for men with low levels. Likewise treating a man with normal levels is unrewarding, however much he might want it to work. In these cases, there is usually another condition causing the symptoms. Such men will be disappointed if they see it as a panacea. I usually prefer to adopt the Ed Miliband (remember him) approach of under-promising and over-delivering. In my own study of nearly 1000 men with type 2 diabetes, we have shown numerous health benefits and reduced mortality over a 10-year period. To date we have published over 14 peer reviewed papers from this research. Men with type 2 diabetes also have high rates of ED, up to 75%, and up to 40% have low testosterone levels. The benefits of screening and treating these men are well established. A 10 -year study from Germany has shown that testosterone can halt progression to diabetes and often reverse type 2 diabetes. These findings support those from the T4DM trial, a large study from Australia, described earlier.

In the US and UK, we face an epidemic of pain-killer abuse. In many cases these drugs may be prescribed for legitimate reasons such as chronic back pain, but low Testosterone levels will be seen in 40-50% of men and they are at higher risk of early death. A recent US study showed a huge reduction in mortality when low T is treated. The advice must be to try to wean off opiate products, even codeine and tramadol, switching to safer drugs such as paracetamol of ibuprofen. This group of patients with low testosterone definitely benefit from testosterone therapy.

By far the most difficult group are men who abuse anabolic steroids (AS) either currently or in the past. All men might have been tempted to try shortcuts in that search for that perfect body that they think women desire. They probably intend to use them for a short time but soon get trapped into ever increasing doses by the rebound symptoms as the levels fall. As some of the doses are several times more than the therapeutic dose, problems can arise very quickly. Acute dangers include thickening of the blood and heart attacks due to raised cholesterol and direct toxic effects on the heart. There are a few very sad cases. The major problems appear a few years later, when the pituitary gland fails to bounce back once the high dose steroids are stopped. By now, the man might be married or wanting to start a family. Often the problem is difficult to diagnose as the man denies past use because of intense shame or fear of being blamed as a "cheat". This is often compounded by endocrinologists who tell men to be patient and wait years for things will recover, even at the cost of their marriage and loss of the best years of their lives. It is very difficult for these men to access sympathetic treatment from recognised specialists and they often drift back into their habit. For those of us who treat them, they can be very demanding, but often rewarding. They often expect the immediate "highs" that they experienced from their previous rapid acting injections, but with patience they can usually be established on safer medications that maintain levels in the normal range, plus, of course, daily tadalafil to treat their ED.

There are often associated infertility problems associated with past AS use, or the treatment now being given. Often, they require regular injections of a drug called HCG (human chorionic gonadotrophin) or an oral drug called clomiphene. Frequently we need to work with fertility specialists to retrieve sperm from the testes and then later proceed to IVF.

If only men commencing AS for that perfect body knew what was waiting for them down the road! The advice here is clear – Do not take them.

The Female Perspective

In the case of Female Sexual Dysfunction, the problem is even more complicated. When companies identified an unmet clinical need, with high levels of distress, this was met by a media reaction that "Bad Pharma" were inventing a disease merely to sell more drugs. The experience with the first drug for women, Flibanserin, in the US has made companies very wary of investing any funding in this area of research. There is still much off-label use of testosterone gels in menopausal women and it is likely that we will eventually see UK licensed product available. As a rule of thumb, the dose required in woman is around 10% of the male dose. Low dose Testosterone therapy can be highly effective for several distressing symptoms not effectively treated by conventional HRT. Working with Dr Louise Newson at the menopause clinic in Stratford-on-Avon and seeing the results of combination of HRT with "off label" testosterone gel, there is no doubt that this treatment transforms lives. There is considerable potential to use daily tadalafil for even better results in women. Effectively treating the woman often unmasks problems in the male partner and enables us to deal with the couple and achieve better results.

In this short chapter, I have tried to bring together some serious issues from my work over the last 30 years and offer some positive advice to readers as to what they can do to improve their heath and their personal happiness. For any physicians reading this book, I can totally recommend a career in Sexual Medicine.

Hopefully, the next Sex Tsar is out there somewhere.

www.ingramcontent.com/pod-product-compliance
Ingram Content Group UK Ltd.
Pitfield, Milton Keynes, MK11 3LW, UK
UKHW041954190726
13854UKWH00005B/1965

9 781913 704315